ASTROLOGY

AND

THE EDGAR CAYCE READINGS

by

Margaret H. Gammon

A.R.E. PRESS ● VIRGINIA BEACH ● VIRGINIA

Printed in the U.S.A.

Acknowledgments

The writer wishes to acknowledge with deep gratitude the assistance of Gladys and Albert Turner for their cooperation in research and making available copies of pertinent readings; to Mary Ann Woodward for her help in research; to Kenneth Broman for his help in setting up a number of birth charts where accurate birth times were known.

To many other A.R.E. members, the writer is indebted for encouragement, criticism and suggestions; a few of these are Lydia J. Schrader Gray, Juliet Ballard, Eula Allen, Jeffrey Furst, Everett Irion and Hugh Lynn Cayce.

Margaret H. Gammon

THE WORK OF EDGAR CAYCE TODAY

The Association for Research and Enlightenment, Inc. (A.R.E.®), is a membership organization founded by Edgar Cayce in 1931.

- 14,256 Cayce readings, the largest body of documented psychic information anywhere in the world, are housed in the A.R.E. Library/Conference Center in Virginia Beach, Virginia. These readings have been indexed under 10,000 different topics and are open to the public.

- An attractive package of membership benefits is available for modest yearly dues. Benefits include: a journal and newsletter; lessons for home study; a lending library through the mail, which offers collections of the actual readings as well as one of the world's best parapsychological book collections, names of doctors or health care professionals in your area.

- As an organization on the leading edge in exciting new fields, A.R.E. presents a selection of publications and seminars by prominent authorities in the fields covered, exploring such areas as parapsychology, dreams, meditation, world religions, holistic health, reincarnation and life after death, and personal growth.

- The unique path to personal growth outlined in the Cayce readings is developed through a worldwide program of study groups. These informal groups meet weekly in private homes.

- A.R.E. maintains a visitors' center where a bookstore, exhibits, classes, a movie, and audiovisual presentations introduce inquirers to concepts from the Cayce readings.

- A.R.E. conducts research into the helpfulness of both the medical and nonmedical readings, often giving members the opportunity to participate in the studies.

For more information and a color brochure, write or phone:

A.R.E., Dept. C., P.O. Box 595
Virginia Beach, VA 23451, (804) 428-3588

TABLE OF CONTENTS

HOW ASTROLOGY ENTERED INTO THE READINGS

Prior to 1923 Edgar Cayce spent over twenty years giving physical readings without any mention or commentary on the subjects of astrology, philosophy or metaphysics.

Then in Dayton, Ohio a man named Arthur Lammers, who was interested in Cayce's work and who had devoted considerable study to philosophy and comparative religions, suggested some non-routine questions be posed to the sleeping Cayce. The answers which came through proved a major surprise for the Cayce family, and served as the basis for a new type of clairvoyant discourse — the life reading. A more detailed story of this is related in the biography *There Is A River,* by Thomas Sugrue.

It should be noted that Cayce was throughout his lifetime a devout Christian and a Sunday school teacher. He had no background whatever in astrology or religious philosophy beyond his own fundamental biblical beliefs.

Consequently, the comments which came through life readings on such subjects as planetary sojourns, akashic records, and past incarnations, were decidedly alien to the waking Cayce's manner of thinking. Nevertheless, the life readings were pursued from 1923 onward, and comprise a major portion of the material in the Cayce files.

Any study of the life readings provides the reader with numerous references to planetary and astrological influences. How these compare with traditional concepts of astrology will rest largely upon the reader's own background and knowledge of the subject.

It should be noted from the beginning, however, that traditional astrological thought maintains, "The stars incline, they do not compel." This view was fully reiterated by Cayce.

The strongest force used in the destiny of man is the sun first, then the closer planets to the earth, or those that are coming to ascension at the time of the birth of the individual, *but let it be understood here, no action of any planet, or the phases of the sun, the moon or any of the heavenly bodies surpass the rule of man's willpower.* **3744-3**

Or, as he stated again and again, "Mind is ever the builder."

What, then, are the planetary influences? What should the study of astrology be concerned with? And if we are not compelled, how are we inclined by our planetary relationships?

To understand fully the complexities of traditional astrology requires considerable study and years of carefully applied experience. Consequently, no complete summary of that subject in comparison with the life readings will be accomplished by this brief text, which can serve only as a springboard to additional research in the combined fields.

With this in mind, our hope is that students of parapsychology and astrologers alike may approach the body of information within the readings with open minds, since there are questions that arise which are not easily resolved.

The major variance, or addition, as it exists within the readings, is based upon the concept of reincarnation and its relationship to various planetary influences. These influences are indicated to be the result of planetary relationships developed during or between previous lives. In fact, of the 2,500 life readings which Cayce gave from 1923 to 1945, almost all refer to past incarnations and specific astrological or planetary influences bearing upon the present.

Past earth experiences, according to the readings, express themselves through an individual's emotions — while at the same time the individual's mental aspects are shown as being developed from dwelling in planes of consciousness (represented by planets) between earth lives. Planetary relationships are thus explained as being symbolic of these experiences and the development achieved. Consequently, each individual varies considerably not only in mental and emotional traits, but also in the manner or degree that a given planet or planetary configuration affects that person.

In brief, planetary relationships are explained as being part of a great plan for soul development, which will be covered in more detail in the following chapters. This plan calls for the individual soul-entity to experience creation in all its diversity, so that each may return as a companion with the Creator.

The record of this experience becomes that part of an individual known as the akasha or soul record. It was these akashic records that the subconscious mind of Edgar Cayce was able to scan and comment upon through the life readings.

The record of planetary influences found in the akasha was explained as being emblematic of how an individual had reacted to various mental and emotional situations in the past. This was shown to be a present and continually evolving relationship:

"As to whether a soul is developed or retarded during a particular life depends on what the person holds as its ideal, and what it does in its mental and material relationships about that ideal.

"Life is a purposeful experience, and the place in which a person finds himself is one in which he may use his present abilities, faults, failures, virtues, in fulfilling the purpose for which the soul decided to manifest in the three-dimensional plane.

"Know in thyself that there are immutable laws, and the universe about thyself is directed by laws set in motion from the beginning.

"So, as ye condemn, so are ye condemned. As ye forgive, so may ye be forgiven. As ye do unto the least of thy brethren, so ye do it unto thy Maker. These are laws; these are truths; they are unfailing. And because He may often appear slow, in meting out results does not alter or change the law. An error, a fault, a failure, must be met. Though the heavens, the earth, may pass away, His word will not pass away. His word is the way, the truth, the light. Each soul must pay to the last jot or tittle."*

Another intriguing aspect of Cayce's commentaries on planetary influences is found in response to a question on the validity of individuals' astrological charts.

For in about twenty percent of the populace at the present time [1933], it is dependent upon what the individuals have done with their urges *through* material sojourns.

As indicated through this channel, some are in keeping with the astrological charts, others are found to be partially so, others are diametrically opposed to same — because of the activities of the individuals.   5753-3

In short, Cayce at times both agreed or disagreed in part with traditional astrology. However, within the realm of his planetary discourses on soul development he presented implications that astrological matters are far more important than our scientifically oriented 20th century minds have allowed us to consider.

Before going to the readings' further explanation of akashic records and soul development, it would be well to note typical examples of entire readings with their planetary references. These have been included for study in Appendix I. For those unfamiliar with astrological terms an additional Appendix (II) and Glossary are provided.

These examples give rise to numerous questions and possibilities for further study of subconscious psychic soul forces. It is toward that "great study," as the readings phrased it (3744), that this introduction is dedicated.   *Jeffrey Furst*

There Is a River by Thomas Sugrue, Chapter on "Philosophy."

Chapter One
THE LANGUAGE OF THE READINGS

A continuing problem occurs in understanding and interpreting the language and various terms found in the readings, several examples of which will be explained here. Additional short definitions will be found in the glossary.

Personality and Individuality

The dictionary makes a very slight distinction between the meanings of these two words, saying that personality is individuality, and that an individual is one who "exists as a single, separate thing or being; separate and particular."

In the readings we are introduced to the novel idea that personality is one thing and individuality is another; further, that they may harmonize or be quite at variance with each other. Here the difference between these two is clearly stated:

As to the appearances in the earth, not all may be given, but as a pattern may be indicated in the personality and individuality of this individual entity. Personality is that ye wish others to think and see. Individuality is that your soul prays, your soul hopes for, desires. They need not necessarily be one; but their purpose must be one, even as the Father, the Son and the Holy Spirit are one. So must body, mind and soul be one in purpose and in aim . . . 5246-1

We are reminded here of the conflicts so often uncovered by psychiatrists, and by implication we suppose that everybody has these conflicts. Yet we also know of many people whom we call "well-balanced," and this must surely mean that their personalities and individualities are in harmony. Are they born with this harmony or do they achieve it? The readings indicate both. Balance comes from constant effort, through application of an ideal in every department of action and thought, including, probably, sojourns in planetary dimensions.

Students of orthodox astrology may parallel the meaning of the ascending sign and its degree with the Sun's position, to understand

1

personality and individuality better. The Ascendant is thought of as pertaining to outside appearance and traits; the Sun in its sign is the inmost self, the spark of the Creator which, individualized, has a purpose for coming to earth in that particular sign. Ideally, one would reflect and support the other, in a harmonious unity or balance.

Thus, as is indicated, may the individuality that is the entity be brought [into] its activities so that its personality may contribute to the factors necessary to keep this entity in the direction needed.   5398-1

The individuality is the sum total of what the entity has done about those things that are creative or ideal in its varied experiences in the earth.   4082-1

What happens when the personality and individuality are not in harmony, or in the process of being harmonized? For one thing, that entity is not influenced by his planetary sojourns.

Urges termed astrological would be very far from correct in this particular entity . . . the personality and the individuality of the entity are quite at variance . . . There is very seldom those that the entity takes into its closest confidence. These bring for the entity that which has been indicated, of a loneliness much, and with even those the entity holds most dear.   5246-1

Few people, few individual souls really enjoy the companionship of themselves. Not merely because they love themselves the less or that they despise themselves the more. But their thoughts and . . . the emotions of the body, are seldom in accord one with the other — or their individuality and their personality don't reflect the same shadow in the mirror of life.   3351-1

This discussion of personality and individuality is very pertinent to the study of the total plan of soul evolution, as described in the readings. According to this concept, between earth lives the soul-entity dwells, or sojourns, in planetary dimensions as a state of consciousness. From these sojourns come the mental urges that are carried over into earth lives, becoming a part of the individuality of the entity which is then expressed in the material world. The previous earth experiences create emotional urges, becoming the entity's personality in the earth lives.

The shadows of those things from the sojourns of this entity in Mercury, Jupiter, Saturn, Uranus, Venus and the influences of the general system's activity as in the Sun and Moon, have their portion [influence] in the very relationships and activity of the entity. These [astrological influences] are but the mental urges that arise, and become the individuality of an entity in expression in the material world; while the appearances in the earth through the various sojourns that are become active in the experience . . . at any one given place or position or appearance or period, are as but the personality in the entity's experience . . . and are as the urges from the emotions that have been created.   633-2

2

Latent and Manifested

Readings often started out by saying:

Yes, we have the entity and those relations with the universe and the universal forces, as are latent in the present experience.   759-1

Or:

While these [urges] are rather given as a composite picture of latent and manifested characteristics, these should be taken into consideration by those about the entity.   305-3

Latent means to lie hidden or concealed, undeveloped within a person or thing, as a quality or power as yet unrevealed. Manifested, then, means the opposite of latent; it suggests a trait or trend — good, bad, or indifferent — currently developing and being revealed.

It's clear that all the latent qualities, talents, etc., are also innate, but the words are not synonymous. Probably all adults have innate qualities which are latent and non-manifested, as well as innate-manifested, and in the making of these possibilities, the planets or planetary sojourns have had a definite and cooperative influence. We ourselves have made these potentials, weaving them in and out, creatively or destructively, from earthly emotional urges and from the planetary mental urges carried over from realms of consciousness outside the earth.

We find that there are those urges latent and manifested, in the personalities and individuality of this entity.

Personalities in the material plane arise from the application of the entity's urges in earthly sojourns. Individualities arise from what an entity would [do] or does about the entity's ideal in a material experience or sojourn in the earth.   3211-2

Aspects

This is a familiar word to students of astrology. Textbooks list major and minor aspects, the major ones being the conjunction, the opposition, the square, the trine and the sextile.

Webster defines aspects in astrology to mean "the position of stars in relation to each other, or to the observer."

In this matter of aspects, the readings diverge rather drastically from textbook astrology. Aspects between planets in the natal chart, or in the sunrise chart, are seldom mentioned or given significance. From a study of hundreds of life readings, we found only one or two in which major aspects were mentioned. Aspects in connection with cycles in a person's life were referred to at times, with the explanation that such aspects involved the primary or secondary planets and thus stirred them to action.

3

Let us cite some extracts showing instances in which aspects between natal planets do not seem to be important.

As to the astrological aspects, we find Jupiter as combined with Venus, Saturn and Uranus being the greater influences.   1931-1

In this chart, there are no major aspects between these planets. Jupiter is at 8 Leo, Venus at 20 Virgo (44 degrees between). Saturn at 2 Virgo, and Uranus at 29 Aquarius. The term Jupiter "as combined with" Venus, Saturn and Uranus seems to have a special meaning, but not in reference to a conjunction.

In the astrological aspects we find the entity headstrong from Mercury, yet very demure in its headstrongness, and oft sets itself to have its way — eventually has it and finds it isn't what was wanted at all. These [conditions] arise from those conflicting influences from Mercury, with Saturn.
Hence many changes in the aspects . . .   1406-1

From the use of the word *conflicting*, and Mercury with Saturn, we would expect a square or an opposition between Mercury and Saturn. This is not the case. Mercury is at 4 Aquarius and Saturn at 20 Libra; which is not close enough to be considered in trine, or 120 degrees, as astrology is taught. These two are 104 degrees apart, and orthodox astrology would not interpret these as interfering one with the other.

Other examples could be cited, but let us consider a reading which may explain what aspects really mean as far as present influences are concerned.

Thus we find that the sojourns about the earth, during the interims between earthly sojourns, are called the astrological aspects. Not that an entity may have manifested physically on such planets, but in that consciousness which is the consciousness of that environ. And these [consciousnesses] have been accredited with certain potential influences in the mental aspect of an entity.   2144-1

That absent from the material body is manifested in what we call astrological aspects, that become a phase of each and every soul — and are signposts along the individual way . . . all of these are a part of thy heritage, thy innate urge; that arises from, and produces influences in, the material experiences in the present.   1745-1

As to urges arising from astrological aspects, or sojourns and activities when absent from materiality — we find these coming from the Moon, Mercury and Uranus.   2459-1

Traditional aspects between planets in the birth chart give little or no clue as to which important planets will exert the most influence as indicated by the readings. A study of the most important

4

planets mentioned in 150 children's readings shows that it is more than likely that there will be no orthodox astrological aspects between any of them.

Yet there seems to be considerable truth in the traditional belief in favorable and unfavorable aspects between planets. This is supported by the readings' own occasional mention and agreement with favorable trines or unfavorable squares when certain planets make these aspects by transit to natal planets (see examples in Appendix).

At the same time, a soul which has stayed out of earthly incarnations for hundreds of years still apparently has many opportunities to encounter favorable and unfavorable aspects to its dwelling-place in the planetary dimensions. According to the way it has learned to handle these inter-planetary vibrations, it comes to earth with various aspects — trines or squares, conjunctions, oppositions, or sextiles. Then, when in the earth the transiting planets attune to this pattern, the opportunity is given that entity to translate into three-dimensional action and reaction, good or bad, to consolidate or to shatter the pattern, to progress in soul growth, or to go backward.

Chapter Two

AKASHA: THE SOUL'S RECORD OF
EVOLUTIONARY PROGRESS

The Cayce life readings are unique in that a great part of the entire soul record, apparently, was scanned and commented upon during the reading. However, only a few planetary sojourns and previous earth lives were given for an individual, with selections made on the basis of what was influencing this particular life to the greatest extent.

How Cayce arrived at that point of being conscious of another individual's soul record was explained in a dream experience which he had twelve to fifteen times while giving readings. Here is one such description, as given by Cayce in the background material for 294-19:

"I see myself as a tiny dot out of my physical body, which lies inert before me. I find myself oppressed by darkness and there is a feeling of terrific loneliness. Suddenly, I am conscious of a white beam of light. As this tiny dot, I move upward following the light, knowing that I must follow it or be lost.

"As I move along this path of light, I gradually become conscious of various levels upon which there is movement. Upon the first levels there are vague, horrible shapes, grotesque forms such as one sees in nightmares. Passing on, there begin to appear on either side mis-shapen forms of human beings with some part of the body magnified. Again there is change and I become conscious of gray-hooded forms moving downward. Gradually, these become lighter in color. Then the direction changes and these forms move upward — and the color of the robes grows rapidly lighter. Next, there begin to appear on either side vague outlines of houses, walls, trees, etc., but everything is motionless. As I pass on, there is more light and movement in what appear to be normal cities and towns. With the growth of movement I become conscious of sounds, at first indistinct rumblings, then music, laughter, and singing of birds. There is more and more light, the colors become very beautiful, and there is

6

the sound of wonderful music. The houses are left behind, ahead there is only a blending of sound and color. Quite suddenly, I come upon a hall of records. It is a hall without walls, without a ceiling, but I am conscious of seeing an old man who hands me a large book, a record of the individual for whom I seek information."

Much is written about Akashic records in metaphysical literature, and the emphasis is usually placed upon that part having to do with earth life. The Cayce readings make it quite clear that each soul is constantly adding to his record, whether he is "in the earth" or in planetary dimensions.

A typical reading starts:

Yes, we have the entity here, and those records that are a part of the entity's experience through the earth's plane, as well as through those interims of sojourn in the environs about the earth.   1990-3

The Akasha is not necessarily a total record of the individual's deeds mixed in with the whole of humanity, although a nation, as an entity, might have its own record. In fact, the Cayce readings indicate that this is true. The individual's soul record is his own and like no other's.

Each soul, each body, each individual, is an individual entity; that done and that thought, becomes as a living record of the experience of that individual entity in whatever sphere of consciousness this activity may be and is recorded upon the skein of time and space.   1292-1

In giving, then, the astrological influences, these would vary considerably from that as would be seen from the spiritual – or the . . . soul-experience in the earth's plane. Were this entity's experiences given from the purely astrological science, as accepted in many quarters, these would vary entirely from this [record] which may be given here, or that is viewed from here – for these are the Akashian records of the entity's or soul's development. As to how the present experience, with its environs, will be acted upon or influenced . . . [there will be] little influence from the astrological standpoint. The entity will be governed rather by the reactions of the experiences in the earth's plane through its appearances, rather than astrological influences.   566-1

Here we see that all individuals are not affected equally by the planets. Some are more influenced than others; some few are not influenced at all. This latter situation is unusual, and we will come back to it.

The Will is the Weaver

If there are two outlines in the record for each individual soul, how exactly do the two sets of influences function in the soul now incarnated in the earth? Of what do the influences consist? The following extracts explain:

Thus in giving interpretations of the records here, we would give not only the environmental but also the hereditary influences; not merely from the material lineage but from the mental and spiritual. For these, too, are a part of the heritage of each and every soul.

While there are those influences [from the planets] those urges latent and manifested, know that no urge surpasses the will of the entity — that birthright given each soul that it may know itself to be itself, and by choice become one with the Creator . . .

For, each soul, each entity *is* a co-creator with the universal consciousness; making those activities for self, for others . . .

For the astrological sojourns represent the mental or dream forces; while the material earthly sojourns represent the expression through the emotions — or the reaction of same in expression, in experiences that may be had, may be sought, may be shunned by the entity.   2571-1

Or, stated in a different manner:

It should be understood that the earthly sojourn urges [pertain] to the emotions, while the mental or innate urges are from the experiences of the soul in the environs about the earth.

But these are merely urges or inclinations, not impelling forces, and these used in their proper relationships as warnings, or as those things to embrace, may be applied in the experience for helpful forces and influences.

Know, however, that it is what the will does about that which is set as its ideal in a mental, in a material or in the physical experiences as well as spiritual — and then having the courage to carry out that ideal — [that] makes the difference between constructive and creative forces or relationships and those that make one become rather as a drifter or ne'er-do-well, or one very unstable and unhappy.   1401-1

To summarize: it seems that the emotions and the senses of the physical body are inherited by the entity from itself, from certain previous lives selected by the soul to manifest in this life. These emotions and sensory reactions make up our "personalities" (as differing from individualities) to be used in this life. Mental awarenesses, intuitions and judgment of right and wrong come to be a part of the body because of the soul's life in spheres of consciousness outside the earth, or in planetary dimensions. Suspended over both, independent of both, is the will which is free to use all factors at its command, either constructively or destructively. It has been suggested that the signs of the zodiac are karmic patterns; the planets are the looms; the will is the weaver.

The entity's task in this life is to use his will to harmonize the two patterns, earth and planetary urges, into a well-rounded whole. This does not mean scorning the material life and rejecting the emotional urges. It means making use of them, spiritualizing them, and making choices of conduct according to the entity's own ideal of what is constructive for himself and others.

Apparently free will is carried over into planetary sojourns after passing from this life. But no matter how high the development is carried in these realms of other consciousness, the plan of soul evolution seems to call for the entity coming into earth life and manifesting the development according to this concept. The earth and our planetary-solar system was specifically designed to be a practice-place for our thorough learning of free will's power. Reading 1719-1 states that astrological influences bring will into the experience in earth — probably by natal planetary relationships (the birth chart) and by transits. It calls will "that factor which may be trained, just as the mental forces are trained," and "the developer in material force" on the earth, or as a balance-wheel between the earth urges and the innate soul urges.

Free Will in Other Dimensions

Many philosophers have doubted that the soul has free will in other dimensions, yet the readings have stated that will is manifested and applied in constructive ways outside the earth.

For Life is a continuous experience. And the mind, the soul, the will, are those influences that act through material manifestation for the improvement, the development, or for retardment to the whole of the experience.

For each soul enters each experience for a development, that it may be prepared to dwell with that which it seeks as its goal.

Hence the necessity of each entity . . . [to set] its ideal in each experience.

Hence we find in the developments through those activities of an entity in a material sojourn or through an astrological experience are but the evolution, or making practical. For it is not what an individual or an entity may proclaim that counts, but what each soul . . . does about that it has set as its ideal in relationships to . . . individuals about same.   1235-1

Yet may this entity be set apart. For through its experiences in the earth, it has advanced from a low degree to that which may not even necessitate a reincarnation in the earth. Not that it has reached perfection but there are realms for instruction if the entity will hold fast to that ideal . . . Remember, there are material urges and there are materials in other consciousnesses not three-dimensions alone.   5366-1

Thus we find this entity – as each entity – is in the present the result of that the entity has applied of Creative influences and forces in every phase of its experience. Thus it makes for that called by some karma, by others racial hereditary forces.

And thus environment and hereditary forces are in their reality the activities of the *mind* of the entity in its choices through the experiences in the material, in the mental, in the spiritual planes.   1796-1

Emotions and the Glandular Centers

Emotions, our inheritance from sojourns in the earth, are complicated by their tie-in with the glandular structure. The following excerpt suggests that a distinction be made.

The awarenesses are a pattern of that we call astrological aspects. Not because the entity in a physical consciousness sojourned in any of the planets which are a part of this present solar experience, but each planet is credited with certain environmental influences that are represented in the characteristics of each individual soul.

Thus, as we find in this entity, they [the planets] give expression in the abilities which find manifestation in the material body through developments or attunements in the glandular system of the body *for* material expression.

Thus upon the skein of time and space is the record of each soul made. In patience, in persistence such a record may be read . . .

As to the appearances or sojourns in the earth – these we find expressed or manifested in the material body through the senses. Do understand and do interpret the differences between the emotions that arise from the sensory system and those that arise from the *glandular* system alone. True, physically these interchange; yet one [the glandular] represents the whole of the development, the other [sensory] represents the step-by-step activity by an entity in its activity through the material world.   2620-2

The Akashic record is embodied in the glandular system for the purpose of the entity's material expression "in patience, in persistence." The practice of meditation arouses the seven glandular centers if and when the purpose is to draw nearer to the Divine source. These centers are the connection between the physical, the mental and the spiritual in man.

The spiritual contact is through the glandular forces or creative energies . . . Thus we find the connection, the association of the spiritual being with the mental self, at those centers from which reflexes react to all of the organs, all of the emotions, all of the activities of a physical body.   263-13

For a more detailed study of meditation, the endocrine glands, and their physical-spiritual connections, see the booklet *Meditation –*

Gateway to Light. * Each of the seven glands, or psychic centers, is said to be attuned or related to a planet, as follows:

The Pituitary (Jupiter)
The Pineal (Mercury)
The Thyroid (Uranus)
The Thymus (Venus)
The Adrenals (Mars)
The Lyden (Neptune)
The Gonads (Saturn)

These relationships and many others were brought out in a series of readings (281) explaining the symbology of the Book of the Revelation of St. John the Divine.

*By Elsie Sechrist, A.R.E. Press, 1964

Chapter Three
THE GREAT PLAN OF SOUL EVOLUTION

The word *cosmogony* is used to describe theories of the physical origin or generation of the universe, and many respectable scientists indulge in such conjecture. Their theories vary, but guesses concerning the unknown are considered academically acceptable when scientists are guessing.

Cosmology, on the other hand, means the philosophy of the nature and first principles of the universe. Physical scientists generally decline to comment on these unknowns, leaving such speculation to philosophers, and calling it metaphysics. But why was the universe made? What is the meaning behind the creation of so many suns and solar systems, stars, galaxies, nebulae? What is the purpose of our own solar system? Are there others with the same purpose? What is the relationship of our own solar system to others? And most important to us: what is man's relationship to these various systems? Or why, essentially, does man exist?

These are questions that preoccupy the philosopher and theologian alike, and the answers are suggested in the life readings given by Edgar Cayce. In these records, man's relationship to the solar system is shown as a plan for soul evolution that is vast and inspiring in scope. According to this information, man is very personally related to his limited universe, our solar system. He is caught up in its purpose, and it is involved in his purpose for being here. There is interaction between man on earth and the planets, sun and moon. He influences them, they influence him. This influence is somewhat different from what is taught by traditional astrology.

For man to know something of this plan is to understand himself and others better. Here, the principles of the Christian ethic become intensified and very personal in meaning. Thus, all men can be seen truly as brothers involved in the struggle for soul evolution and growth. Our solar system was created for mankind's evolution.

As has been indicated by some, ye are part and parcel of a universal consciousness or God — and thus all that is within the universal consciousness, or the universal awareness; as the stars, the planets, the sun, the moon. Do ye rule them or they rule thee? They were made for thy own use, as an individual – yea, that is the part, the thought which thy Maker, thy Father-God thinks of thee.

For ye are as a corpuscle in the body of God; thus a co-creator with Him, in what ye think, in what ye do.   2794-3

The next reading becomes more specific about the influence of our solar system:

When the heavens and the earth came into being, this meant the universe as the inhabitants of the earth know same; yet there are many suns in the universe – even those about which our sun, our earth, revolves; and all are moving toward some place – yet space and time appear to be incomplete.

Then time and space are but one. Yet the sun, that is the center of this particular solar system, is the center; and, as has been indicated and known of old, it [the sun] is that about which the earth and its companion planets circulate or revolve.

The beginnings of the understanding of these, and their influences upon the lives of individuals, were either thought out, evolved, or interpreted by those of old, without the means of observing same as considered today necessary in order to understand.

Astronomy is considered a science, and astrology as foolishness. Who is correct? One [astronomy] holds that because of the position of the earth, the sun, the planets, they are balanced one with another in some manner, some form; yet that they have nothing to do with man's life or the expanse of life, or the emotions of the physical being in the earth.

Then, why and how do the effects of the sun *so* influence other life in the earth and not affect *man's* life, man's emotions?

As the sun has been set as the ruler of this solar system, does it not appear to be reasonable that it *has* an effect upon the inhabitants of the earth, as well as upon plant and mineral life in the earth? . . .

Thus as we find given [in the Bible], the sun and the moon and the stars were made also – this being the attempt of the writer to convey to the individual the realization that there *is* also an influence in their activity! For, remember, they – the sun, the moon, the planets – have their marching orders from the divine, and they move in same.

Man alone is given that birthright of free will. He alone may defy his God!
5757-1

Thus we come to the idea of man as a possible and actual rebel, with the need for this awareness as part of his soul evolution; hence the need for the solar system, for earth lives and planetary sojourns. Man's defiance and rebellion came about when "souls projected themselves into matter (earth) and became aware that they had the

13

ability to create, responsibly or irresponsibly, without the spirit of truth." They became more and more material-minded, or selfish, and lost the feeling of oneness with the Father; the pattern was flawed — the purpose for which they had been created — to be companions with the Father. Souls had to start the long way back to Him, learning to use their minds and wills in creative instead of selfish ways, with love instead of hate, with patience and faith instead of hasty judging. These virtues were to be applied to self, in guiding one's thoughts and actions inward, as well as toward other souls.

The earth became a "practice place" where souls were to demonstrate what they had learned in other lives, combined with lessons from other dimensions of consciousness, represented by the planets when absent from the earth in these other dimensions. Each planet represented a portion of these lessons to be learned — each a cluster of spheres or planes or vibratory dimensions of consciousness in which the soul was to dwell and become aware.

The very natures or influences from the elemental forces themselves were drawn in those activities of the elements within the earth, that could give off their vibrations because of the influences that attracted or drew away from one another.

This was produced by that which had come into the experiences in materiality, or into being, as the very nature of water with the sun's rays; or the ruler of thy own little solar system, thy own little nature in the form ye may see in the earth!

Hence we find how, as ye draw your patterns from these, that they become a part of the whole. For ye are *relatively* related to all that ye have contacted in materiality, mentality, spirituality! All of these are a portion of thyself in the material plane.

In taking form they become a mental body with its longings for its home, with right and righteousness.

Then that ye know as thy mental self is the form taken, with all of its variations as combined from the things it has been within, without, and in relationship to the activities in materiality as well as in the spheres or various consciousnesses . . .   5755-1

Man Affects the Solar System

Listeners to reading 5757-1 felt many questions in their minds and hearts about man's disobedience really affecting the solar system. In answers to their questions, the reading proceeded to amplify many points. The sun, it stated, was made for the purpose of shedding light and heat upon God's children in the earth, and is of the same composition of which man is made: solid, liquid and vapor, or the various stages of consciousness or activity for man. Describing the sun's stability, the reading states it was

. . . commanded to march, to show forth the Lord's glory, His beauty, His mercy, His hope – yea – His patience . . .

Questions were asked about sun spots; the reading calls them

. . . those turmoils and strifes that have been and that are the sin of man . . . reflected upon even the face of the sun . . .

How do they [sun spots] affect man? How does a cross word affect thee? How [do] anger, jealousy, hate, animosity affect thee *as* a son of God? If thou art the father of same, oft ye cherish same. If thou art the recipient of same from others, thy brethren, how does it affect thee? Much as that confusion which is caused upon the earth by that which appears as a sun spot. The disruption of communications of all natures between men . . .

Then, what are the sun spots? A natural consequence of that turmoil which the Sons of God in the earth reflect upon same [the sun].

Thus they oft bring confusion to those who become aware of same . . .

Know that thy mind – thy *mind* – is the builder! As what does thy soul appear? A spot, a blot upon the sun? or as that which giveth light unto those who sit in darkness, to those who cry aloud for hope?   5757-1

Changes in the universe and in the relative positions of planets, stars and Zodiac are attributed to man's activity, good and bad.

As in the studies of the entity it is seen that the soul of man is a mere speck in space, yet the soul – though indefinite – is that vital force or activity which is everlasting. Though the earth, though the stars, may pass away; though there may be changes in the universe as to relative position, these are brought about by those combinations of that speck of human activity as relative to the soul's expression in any sphere of existence.   1297-1

How Can Astrology Help?

In reading 3744, this question was asked: "Is it proper for us to study the effects of the planets on our lives in order to better understand our tendencies and inclinations as influenced by the planets?" The answer was a resounding yes.

When studied aright, very, very, very much so. How aright then? In that influence as is seen in the influence of the knowledge already obtained by mortal man. Give more of that into the lives, giving the understanding *that the will must be the ever guiding factor to lead man on, ever upward.*   3744-3

The part that will plays in man's evolution along the Christ-path toward companionship with God cannot be overemphasized. Man in the earth is like a battleground on which mental and spiritual urges

15

from planetary sojourns meet and vanquish, or harmonize with, the emotional urges from past lives.

The umpire or arbiter in this battle, the General who marshals both sides and directs the outcome, is the will of the soul-entity. Free will is the constant, the God-spark. This fact is reiterated, from many points of view, and in various language, in the following extracts:

... those influences as are seen in the appearances of the entity ... may be altered much, as the astrological influences bring in the experience *of* the entity WILL, that factor which may be trained, even as the mental forces, and WILL, that developer in the material force, being the balance between influences, as to those innately built or those of that karmic influence that makes for the *freedom* of the mental being; for in Truth one finds freedom, for he that findeth the Truth is free indeed.   1719-1

Astrological aspects may or may not become a part of the experience physically for the entity. For these are merely urges, and the will – that which designates God's creation of man from the rest of the animal world – rules as to what an individual soul does with opportunities in relationships with the fellowman.   3340-1

For, will is that factor in the experience of each entity in material mani-festation which gives the ability to choose that as may be for the development or the retardment. For, as has so oft been indicated, there is today – now – set before each and every entity, every soul, that which is life and death, good and evil. Each entity, each soul chooses in its manifestations.   1646-2

Not that there are not definite helps to be attained from astrology, but those who live by same the more oft are controlled rather than controlling ... Astrology is a fact, in most instances. But astrological aspects are but signs, symbols. *No influence* is of greater value or of greater help than the *will* of an individual.

Use such directions [from the planets] as stepping stones. Do not let them become stumbling stones in thy experience.   815-6

It seems reasonable to believe that realms of consciousness through which souls have developed will be reflected, at least partially, in the planetary patterns of their horoscopes. If this is so we can get clues to our mental and spiritual selves by studying this record of choices.

Planets Were Made for Man

Rather, then, than the stars ruling the life, the life should rule the stars – for man was created a little bit higher than all the rest of the whole universe, and is capable of harnessing, directing, enforcing the laws of the universe.   5-2

This plan for man's soul evolution is also stated in the following excerpt:

The earth is the Lord's and the fullness thereof. The universe He called into being for these purposes that the individual soul that might be one with Him, would have, does have those influences for bringing this to pass or to be in the experience of every soul.

For hath it not been given that the Lord thy God hath not willed that any soul should perish? But He hath prepared with every temptation a means, a way of escape.

Hence the position or the period of the entrance [birth] is not ruled by the position [of sun and planets] but it may be judged by the position, as to the influence . . . upon an entity's experience because of the entity's application of self's abilities relative to its position in the universal scheme of things . . . 1347-1

This means that some of the progress, at least, can be judged in reference to the horoscope, with its rising sign and angles, and by a certain number (not all) of the planets. This progress can be judged by the manner in which a soul has applied its abilities previously, "according to the universal scheme of things," or constructively.

Variations Between Horoscope Readings and Life Readings

There is a difference, however, between information derived from a horoscope reading and that from a life reading.

Q-2. What is a horoscope reading?

A-2. That in which the planets and their relative forces [have] to do with the planets that control the actions without respect of will, or without respect of the earthly existences through which the body has passed.

Q-3. Do horoscope readings include former appearances in the earth plane?

A-3. Not at all. The former appearances and the relation of the solar forces in the universe have their relations to what might be termed life readings, or experiences. For, as has been shown and given, horoscope, the science of the solar system and its relation to various phases of earth's existence, may mean for [apply to] anyone. In life existence in earth's plane, and the entity's relation to other spheres, there is a different condition. For the sojourn in other spheres than earth's plane controls more the conditions or the *urge* of the individual. Just as we see in the earth plane an individual is controlled by the surroundings, or by the circumstances that have to do with the individual, yet we find the urge, the latent forces, that would give an individual, or two groups, or two individuals raised under the same environment, of the same blood, different urges. These are received from experiences the spirit entity gains in other spheres, correlated with its present circumstance and condition. These should

17

never be confused. For, to gain a horoscope is only the mathematical calculation of earth's position in the universe at any given time, while in the life reading would be the correlation of the individual with a given time and place, with its relative force as applied and received through other spheres and manifested in earth's sphere in the flesh, and the development being the extenuation of the soul's development manifested in the earth plane through subconscious forces of a body or entity.   254-21

Necessity for Planetary Experiences

Before considering the actual urges from the planets working through man in his daily life, let us consider the question of why there are eight planets, Sun and Moon. We are told in many of the readings that the soul-entity outside the earth plane may even pass on to other solar systems, through Arcturus, Polaris or Septimus, or may choose to return to earth.

. . . though there may be worlds, many universes, even much as to solar systems, greater than our own that we enjoy in the present, this earthly experience or this earth is a mere speck when considered even with our own solar system. Yet the soul of man, thy soul encompasses *all* in this solar system or in others . . .

But hast thou conceived − or canst thou conceive − the requirements of influence to meet all the idiosyncrasies of a *single* soul? How many systems would it require? In thyself ye find oft one friend for this, another for that, another for this relationship, another for the prop, another to arouse. Yet all are the work of His hand, are thine to possess, thine to use . . .

Is God's hand short, that there would not be all that each soul would require?   5755-2

Planetary Dimensions

Various attempts have been made to describe the soul's spiritual dwellings outside the earth plane, or in the interims between death and birth. Some feel that the soul goes directly to some other planet, and manifests there in the same way in which it manifested on the earth plane; that it inhabits each planet, as the material body inhabits the earth.

This is a misconception, according to the readings, and yet it cannot be definitely stated what is meant by planes or spheres, or dimensions of consciousness, or vibratory centers. The earth is a three-dimensional planet, and while we are here, we think mostly in three-dimensional terms. In some dream states, the soul may be in a four-dimensional state. The readings state that there are eight dimensions.

When we speak of the earth being a three-dimensional environment, we mention length, breadth, and thickness. Yet the readings define the three dimensions as "time, space and patience."

For the entity finds itself a body, a mind, a soul — three; or the earth consciousness as a three-dimensional plane in one.

So man's concept of the Godhead is three-dimensional — Father, Son and Holy Spirit. The communication or activity or the motivating force we find is three-dimensional — time, space and patience. Neither of these exists in fact, except in the concept of the individual as it may apply to time or space or patience.   4035-1

Vibrations Explained

We now have a number of terms describing planetary dimensions: spheres, planes, phases of consciousness, stages of the condition, dimensions of consciousness, etc. To these we add the term "vibrations," which is perhaps the most understandable description of all. In the following reading, planetary vibrations are explained by drawing a parallel with the vibrations one collects, absorbs and builds by dwelling and working in a special environment, such as a college.

. . . attending this or that university . . . would make for a parlance peculiar unto itself. Even though individuals may study the same line of thought, one attending Harvard, another Yale, another Oxford, another Stanford, another the University of Arizona, they each would carry with them the vibrations created by their very activity in those environs.

In the same way emotions arise from individual activity in a particular sojourn; and are called the *spirit* of the institution to which the entity may have carried itself . . . So we find those astrological sojourns making these vibrations or impressions in the present entity . . .   633-2

We are affected by planetary vibrations (transits of planets) during our lifetimes because we have attuned ourselves to them during sojourns in those environs. The portion of our personality vibrations represented by a planet's vibrations which we have acquired reacts to the movements of a transiting planet.

This concept of the effect of planets seems to be what is referred to here:

Then there are the sojourns in other realms of the solar system which represent certain attributes. Not that ye maintain a physical earth-body in Mercury, Venus, Jupiter, Uranus or Saturn; but there is an awareness or a consciousness in those realms when absent from the body, and the response to the position those planets occupy in this solar system.

Thus ye oft find in thy experiences that places, peoples, things and conditions are a part of self as if ye were in the consciousness of same. 2823-1

But what has all this to do with the plan of soul evolution?

Each entity is a part of the universal whole. All knowledge, all understanding that has been a part of the entity's consciousness, then, is a part in the entity's experience.

Thus the unfoldment in the present is merely *becoming aware of* that experience through which the entity — either in body or in mind — has passed in a consciousness. 2823-1

Chapter Four

THE PLANETS

For when thou beholdest the glory of the Father in the earth, how *orderly* are all His glories! Hast thou watched the Sun in his orbit? How *orderly* are those places of the inhabitation of the souls of men, even in thine *own* — in thine *own* — understanding of this solar system! How orderly is there brought into manifestation day and night, heat and cold, spring and summer! . . . canst thou — as His son — be more unorderly than He and expect His blessings?
440-14

The readings refer to the planets as vibratory centers or the "places of the inhabitation of the souls of men" between earth lives. Is there awareness in these vibratory centers? The readings indicate that there is.

Thus as the soul passes from the aspects about the material environs, or the earth, we find the astrological aspects are represented as stages of consciousness; given names that represent planets or centers or crystallized activity.
Not that flesh and blood, as known in the earth, dwells therein; but in the consciousness, with the form and manner as befits the environ.   **1650-1**

Also during the interims between such [material] sojourns there are consciousnesses or awarenesses. For, the soul is eternal, it lives on, has a consciousness in the awareness of that which has been builded.   **2620-2**

Reading 5755-1 refers to Uranus' tone or attunement; hence we must add vibration of sound and color to our total concept of planetary dwelling places. Many other readings allude to the vibrations of music and color in reference to the planets.

. . . the tonal vibration is that which *produces* color. For, of course, color and tone are just different rates of vibration.   **2779-1**

For it is not strange that music, color, vibration are all a part of the planets, just as the planets are a part — and a pattern — of the whole universe.   **5755-1**

Specific colors and notes of the scale have been attributed to specific planets but not enough research has been done to cite these here, or even to say that just one color belongs to a given planet. Light and dark red, for instance, are mentioned, as are hues, tinges, mixtures, etc. It could be that the planets' colors form a rainbow in which (to the human eye) one color merges into another. And if each planet represents a musical note of vibration, then there are sharps and flats, chords, melodies, counter-point and symphonies — the "music of the spheres" referred to in the readings.

Because man is equipped to see colors and to hear music, the concept of the planets as centers of vibration seems more satisfactory than the concept of "dimensions" which is also a term used in the readings.

Why are eight vibrations needed in the planetary scheme for soul development?

For, without passing through each and every stage of development, there is not the correct vibration to become one with the Creator . . .

Then, in the many stages of development throughout the universal, or in the great system of the universal forces . . . each stage of development [is] made manifest through flesh, which is the testing portion of the universal vibration. In this manner then, and for this reason, all [are] made manifest in flesh, and [there is] development through the eons of time, space, and [that] *called* eternity.   900-16

The individual who requested the following reading was evidently interested in numerology, as one question asked about having a soul number. The answer stated that only in the earth plane does an entity have a soul number. Another question was whether the entity has an opportunity to change its rate of vibration in planetary sojourns. This was the answer:

Each planetary influence vibrates at a different rate of vibration. An entity entering that influence enters that vibration; [it is] not necessary that he change, but it is the grace of God that he may! It is part of the universal consciousness, the universal law.   281-55

There is a great deal of individual variation in each soul's awarenesses of the planets.

Hence the entity passes along those stages that some have seen as planes, some have seen as steps, some have seen as cycles, and some have experienced as places.   5755-1

Textbooks and the Readings

Astrological textbooks attribute definite and specific meanings as well as influences to the various planets. How do these meanings compare with the readings? There are striking similarities, but also

**EDGAR CAYCE FOUNDATION and
A.R.E. LIBRARY/VISITORS CENTER**
Virginia Beach, Va.
OVER 50 YEARS OF SERVICE

notable differences. These will be pointed out as each planet is discussed. It should be remembered, though, that even the astrologers do not agree on every point.

MERCURY

Textbooks say that Mercury is the planet of mind, reason and intellect; the planet of speech, writing and communication; governs the arms, hands, lungs, tongue, intestines, sense of sight.

Notice that Mercury is associated directly with the other senses as well as sight: with the hands, therefore the sense of touch; with the tongue, therefore sense of taste and the associated sense of smell. The sense of hearing is also attributed to Mercury.

Ellen McCaffery, in her *Graphic Astrology,* * discusses Mercury thus: "Astrology shows us that the planet Mercury governs the mind. We reap our reward according to the way we use our mind. If Mercury comes to the planet Mars [occupies by transit the same degree as Mars in birth-chart], we can use this energy [Mars] to fight people, or we can do some constructive work. If Mercury comes to Saturn, we can be melancholy and mean, or we can use the rays of Saturn to help us delve down into the structure of things. It all depends upon how we discipline our minds, just what we will do when the planets move. The more unevolved the soul, the more it responds to adverse planetary vibration."

The readings repeatedly maintain that "mind is the builder," and this is in accordance with orthodox teachings in astrology. However, a divergence lies in the readings' wider and more comprehensive concepts of the mind of man.

Hence we find the mental body is both finite and infinite, a part of self and yet a part of a universal consciousness — or the mind of the Maker.   1650-1

Mercury brings the high mental abilities; the faculties that at times may become the developing for the soul or at others be turned to the aggrandizement of selfish interests.

For the entity is among those who have entered the earth during those years when there was the great entrance of those who have risen high in their abilities; and who are then passing through those periods when there must be application of the will, else the very abilities that have been maintained in the Sun and Mercurian influences will become as stumbling blocks . . .   633-2

Why is mind the builder? Because it exercises choice between good and evil, or the delicate balance between the most-good with the least-evil. Will motivates that choice, and mind controls will.

*Macoy Publishing Co., Richmond, Va., 1952

23

Mind is the factor that is in direct opposition of will. Mind being that control of, or being the spark of the Maker, the WILL, the individual when we reach the plane of man. 3744-1

Mercury, which symbolizes mental consciousness, is the catalyst by which all eight planetary vibrations are harmonized, harnessed, assimilated and put to full constructive use on the earth plane, if advancement is to be made.

As a matter of fact, it is impossible to consider any one planet entirely apart from the others which influence the dominant one. Note the following explanation of Mercury's role:

In Jupiter's forces we find those great ennobling [elements], those conditions that would bring the monies and the forces of good in the life.

In Neptune, those of the mysticism, mystery, spiritual insight, spiritual development.

The Mercury influence of mental understanding of each.

Then, with the mental insight into the operative elements of ennobling, of virtues, of good, of beautiful, with the mysteries of the universal forces, given understanding, brings the development to soul's forces. For the soul feeds upon that environment to which the mental guides and directs, and the expectancy is that soul development that each entity must exercise through will. 900-14

In the readings, Mercury is associated with the pineal gland.

VENUS

Venus is the earth's closest neighbor, not counting the Moon. McCaffery says it "manifests all the things of the world glorified under the radiance of the Sun. It betokens the principle of love on earth, of attraction, joy, gifts, and benefits." It signifies, at its best, harmony, sweetness, gentleness, and the spirit of refinement and good taste. It encourages man to make his surroundings beautiful, and so governs the arts. In music it rules melody rather than harmony, which pertains more to the mental Mercury. It is the peace-making planet. Books on astrology call Venus "the Lesser Benefic," the planet through which many fortunate and good things come to the individual.

The readings agree with all these concepts of the role of Venus' influence upon the soul-self because of its sojourns in those vibrations. The dominant planet — the one from which the soul took flight to come to earth — will show forth its influence through other planets named as influential in the life reading, and fortunate indeed is the soul which arrived from Venus. Here are a few excerpts:

One of a tender, loving disposition; [who] may be ruled or reasoned with through love, obedience or duty; yet may not be driven . . . through sheer force or fear of punishment.

In this influence also we will find, then, that sympathy — or the activities in being able under any circumstances to make for the alleviating of hardships, pains or such conditions in the experience of others — will ever be *appealing* to the entity.   309-1

In the astrological aspects we find that, through influences from sojourns in the Venus environs, the entity is a lover of beauty; especially of song.

And there should be given training and development, and the awakening for the entity in those influences . . . for the use of the entity's voice in *praise* and in thanksgiving . . .

Hence all things that have to do with phases of man's ability of expression, in beautiful ways and manners will be of interest . . . whether pertaining to nature, to voice or song, or even to art subjects.   1990-3

In the following reading, a significant statement is made regarding beauty and the home, for a child who entered the earth plane through the forces of Venus.

As Venus is the ruling influence in the experience, we find that the home will be, should be, the channel through which the greater abilities . . . may be made manifest.

Not that there are not abilities in music, in art . . . But making an artistic home, making a home that is the expression of beauty in all its phases, is the greater career of *any* individual soul. This [the home] is the closer expression of that which has been manifested in the experiences of man's advent into materiality.   2571-1

Here is an enlarged concept of the influences from Venus' forces, which are primarily love; but love, too, has its extremes.

In Venus the body-form is near to that in the three-dimensional plane. For it is what may be said to be rather *all*-inclusive! For it is that ye would call love — which, to be sure, may be licentious, selfish; which also may be so large, so inclusive as to take on the less of self and more of the ideal, more of that which is giving.

What is love? Then what is Venus? It is beauty, love, hope, charity — yet all of these have their extremes. But these extremes are not in the expressive nature or manner as may be found in the tone or attunement of Uranus [the planet of extremes]; for they (in Venus) are more in the order that they blend as one with another.   5755-1

According to the readings, the gland associated with the planet Venus is the thymus. Some physiologists and pathologists say that this gland has atrophied in the adult body, or at least has shrunk considerably. Could this be a commentary on our lives?

MARS

The next planet beyond the earth is Mars, whose orbit encloses the Sun-Mercury-Venus-Earth group.

Mars is said to be the planet of energy or sex. It rules creativeness, construction, invention, ceaseless activity, force, power, work, strife, war, and death. McCaffery says: "It declares the ceaseless, ever-new stream of energy which brings about new forms; hence it is said to rule the sex energies. When the rays of Mars play upon the Moon, they single out the instinct of pugnacity, anger, and self-assertiveness. Mars can make these into very destructive forces, or it can exalt them into the noblest virtues — courage, strength of character, self-confidence, and power."

Further interpretations of Mars' attributes given in the textbooks are: rulership over adventure, sports activities and businesses; the sense of taste; its stone, the bloodstone; its color, red; its day of the week, Tuesday.

With the majority of these attributes the Cayce readings agree, except that the readings emphasize the *inwardness* or psychological urge of planetary vibrations rather than outward events. For some entities or souls, however, the vibrations of Mars are scarcely felt or easily subdued, because they have mastered the impulses to anger, selfishness and aggression. Such souls may be said to have a "good Mars," as the astrologers would put it. This writer, in examination of dozens of accurate birth charts, has not been able to find that such a good Mars has only good aspects (trine, sextile, etc.). We would conclude that the good attributes of Mars in any present earth-plane existence result from the quick learning of the lessons for which the soul came to earth, lessons inherent in the Mars vibrations.

The following excerpts from the readings delineate the attributes cited above:

Astrologically we find Mars, Mercury, Venus and Jupiter, and note their importance. [The entity entered from Mars.] Anger may upset the body and cause a great deal of disturbance, to others as well as to self.

Be angry, but sin not. You will learn it only in patience and in self-possession.

3621-1

Astrologically we find quite a few variations in the entity's experiences. Besides Mercury we find Neptune, Saturn, and Mars always stepping in. Hence it has appeared to the entity at times that many of the associates . . . can get

26

mad easier than anybody. Yet the entity may be mad and sin not. Righteous anger is a virtue. He that has no temper is very weak; but he who controls not his temper is much worse.   3416-1

For the inclinations from the Martian influences are for anger to arise easily in the experiences when the entity is fraught [frustrated] in its activities, in the associations, in its determinations.

And it usually has its way, unless there is reason and love and care and precaution shown by those that direct the developing or formative periods.
                                                                                    1434-1

Lest we forget that the planetary urges, strong as they may be, cannot and should not rule the life, consider this reading for a four-year-old child. Warnings are given to the parents at the very beginning that the child not be allowed to play with fireworks and firearms, "For, Mars is adverse to Jupiter in the experience."

Astrological aspects may or may not become a part of the experience physically for the entity. For these are merely urges, and the will — that which designates God's creation of man from the rest of the animal world — rules, as to what an individual soul does with opportunities in relationships with the fellowman.

In Mars we find this activity. The entity will never be called lazy. May be called stubborn at times, but this, too, may be directed — not by undue punishment but by reasoning with an appealing to the entity . . . Not that there should be a prize for goodness, but remembering that virtue has its own reward, even in those attempting to direct or train children.   3340-1

In the readings, the gland associated with Mars is the adrenal.

JUPITER

The planet next farther out from Mars, or the third, counting Earth as number one, is Jupiter.

Jupiter is called "the Greater Benefic" in astrology textbooks, and to it are attributed good fortune, wealth, social position, happiness, etc. An astrology magazine gives Jupiter as patron of expansion, gain and optimism; controlling the liver, hips, thighs, sense of smell; its colors, green and purple; its metal, tin; and its gem, the turquoise. McCaffery comes closest to the readings' description of Jupiter, when she says, "The emotions can become beautiful under Jupiter, but they are always expanded in scope. The moon and Venus may express tenderness to one, but Jupiter may express benevolence, kindness, and generosity to everyone . . . Jupiter seeks the cause and basis of actions . . . Because the planet inquires into motives and purposes, it is essentially the planet of the judge and the lawmaker.

Under its rays the moral qualities within man begin to develop. Largeness of outlook is cultivated. There is nothing petty or small about Jupiter. It stands for soul growth, expansion, and magnanimity."

The last two sentences coincide with what the readings say about the inner urge or attunement of the soul which entered the earth plane with Jupiter as one of the affecting planets, and, moreover, affecting it favorably.

Speaking generally, however, the readings stress universality and ennoblement as Jupiter's vibrations, showing how these turn the soul-self towards large groups of people, even nations. The following excerpts show how Jupiter's expansive influence works through the other planets named as affecting the life.

In Venus with Jupiter we see those abilities to appreciate those things and experiences that are as from the realm of the universal consciousness, as indicated in the song of the bird, the music as of the stream, the beauty as of nature; and yet with Jupiter these become universal forces, or those activities in the material plane will have to do with groups and masses, rather than individuals; though it may be individual in its application. 2869-1

From the Jupiterian sojourn we find not only the benevolent but the adverse forces. For, while Venus *with* the Jupiterian brings the enjoyment of the beautiful in ways that would pertain to a universal consciousness or activity, the adverse in Mars indicates that wrath . . . may bring those things that will cause the influence to be in a reverse manner . . . 1990-3

As we find then those influences in the astrological aspects show Jupiter rather as the ruling force. [The entity entered from Jupiter.]

Hence, the entity's activities must have to do with the many . . . Those influences in Venus make for an open, frank, loving disposition; making for friends in most any walk or every walk of life. 1442-1

In the latter reading, Venus and Neptune were cited as secondary and tertiary influences, and Neptune's influences were also described as expansive, showing how Jupiter works through the other important planets.

In another instance the entity was said to have entered the earth plane from Jupiter, with Venus, Mercury and Mars affecting the life. Notice how the urges from Venus, Mercury and Mars are *broadened* in outlook through Jupiter's influence:

In Jupiter we find the great ennobling influences, the broad-mindedness, the ability to consider others, the universal consciousnesses that are a part of the entity's unfoldment.

We find in Venus that unusual attraction that the opposite sex will have for the entity, and the entity for the opposite sex. Hence those relationships in such

28

should be the problems as well as the studies and the guidance, through the periods especially in [the] next cycle − or during the next seven years for the entity.

In Mercury and in Mars we find the energetic activities of mind and of body and at times that appearing . . . [to] others in relationship to the entity as a meddler. Yet these are the benevolent forces, if those activities, those consciousnesses of the entity are used and analyzed in that way of aiding the entity in its preparations through such experiences.   2890-2

A "good Jupiter," say the textbooks, brings money and this world's goods, comfort and perhaps luxury. The readings seem to agree with this.

In Jupiter we find the associations making for those tendencies for large groups to be in relationships with the entity. This makes also for those inclinations that in the experience of the entity will be great amounts of this world's goods. May the training also then not only in its teen-age [years] but throughout its development be as to the use of same [wealth] − as being *lent from Creative Forces and energies* and not as for self-indulgence or aggrandizements.
1206-3

The readings say Jupiter rules the pituitary gland.

SATURN

The concept of Saturn, the fourth planet outward counting the earth as one, is one thing in the textbooks and another in the Cayce readings. Here is one of the greatest discrepancies with traditional astrology. Let us carefully examine the differences.

An astrology magazine says: "Saturn has dominion over age, caution, limitation, stabilization, the bones, spleen, teeth, sense of hearing, head, dark colors, Saturday."

McCaffery says, among other things, that Saturn is the recluse, the scientist, anything highly organized or condensed into capsule form, the principle of contraction and solidification. "Saturn governs organization and, therefore, is said to rule the governments of nations, and the executive bodies of large corporations . . . Saturn gives depth to the character and firmness of conviction. He confers sobriety, prudence, good sense, dependability, and patience . . . Saturn is the Lord of Time; but if you have built the foundation, walls, and roof secure, then Saturn will do you little harm."

Saturn is said to be the planet of love of tradition and opposition to change. It is the ruler of the sign of Capricorn, the natural tenth house of the Zodiac.

No, the readings say: Saturn *rules change!*

29

In Saturn we find the sudden or violent changes – those influences and environs that do not grow, as it were, but are sudden by that of change of circumstances materially, or by activities apparently upon the part of others that become a part of self in the very associations. And yet these are testing periods of thy endurance, of thy patience, of thy love of truth, harmony and the spirit that faileth not.

From the combination of this with Uranus we find the extremes; the environs materially or mentally in which the very opposites may be expected.

Remember, only in Christ, Jesus, do extremes meet.   1981-1

Those who recognize in themselves the tendency to start a lot of projects in which they lose interest and seldom finish, will find this excerpt interesting.

From Saturn we find the tendency for the starting of new experiences, the starting of new associations in the activities; and unless these are tempered with the mental influences they are rarely carried to their full termination. This again should be as a warning to the entity. When thou hast chosen that direction, that activity thou would take, know that thou art kept in a balance that is of material, mental and spiritual influences near to right. Then lay it not aside until it, the activity, has borne fruit in thine mental and material experience.   361-4

The influences in Mars and Saturn show for urges that will develop towards those things pertaining to music [the entity entered from Venus] . . . continually starting this or that activity which has to do or deals with new associations, new relations, new activities . . . of not only self but those about the entity.   324-5

There are dozens of extracts stating specifically that Saturn rules *changes,* and we quote several to reinforce this point:

We find in Saturn many changes in the experience. The entity will ever find itself very opposed to being poor, and would go to almost any length to obtain the material things of life. Let not these, thy good works, be evil spoken of because of material things being considered to such a degree as to disregard others' privileges or obligations.   3205-1

In Saturn we find the inclinations for changes, as to this, that or the other; and to muddle a great many things together in the activity.

Hence that injunction as given by the sages of old, "The merchant is never the student, neither is the student ever the merchant," should be a part of the entity's program in its choice of its activity in this experience.   1426-1

Astrologically we find that Venus, Saturn and Neptune are the urges. Thus these will be found to make many changes, yet the entity is one loving, a friend, one who may be counted on as a friend, or as a foe, to be sincere – if the directions are given properly for the entity during these trying periods.   3806-1

From the next reading we get an inkling of the tradition that Saturn is the great taskmaster, the teacher of patience under adversity:

In the astrological activities that produce or bring about these experiences [desire for travel, change] as innate, we find Uranus, Neptune, Saturn as ruling influences; which make for the interest in yet the fear of occult and mystic forces. But rather if there is the activity and the expression of the *psychic,* rather than occult *or* mystic, we may find greater development, greater experiences for the entity.

For in Uranus we find the extremes, and when the entity is very good it's very, *very* good; when it's bad, it's awful! These become *extremes* then in the experience.

Those then of the experiences must be tempered rather with the activities that come from environmental as well as the expressions of the Venus influence.

While the Venus influences are latent, these should find the greater expression; else the urges as from Saturn would make for the entity having *many* homes, or many marriages — and these are *not* well in the experience if there are to be the developments.

For consistency and persistency are the sister of patience; patience the entity needs to learn as its lesson in this experience.   1431-1

Saturn's Role in Soul Evolution

Besides giving the urge for changes in the earth-plane, Saturn's role in the scheme of soul evolution is one of sorrow and change. To put it another way: the need for changing sends the soul or attracts the soul to Saturn after an earth-life in which too many of God's laws have been misused.

Q-22. What is meant by banishment of a soul from its Maker?

A-22. Of the will as given in the beginning to choose for self as in the earthly plane, all insufficient matter is cast unto Saturn. To work out his own salvation as would be termed in the word, the entity or individual banishes itself, or its soul . . .   3744-2

In the sphere of many of the planets within the same solar system, we find they [entities] are banished to certain conditions in developing about the spheres from which they pass; and again and again and again, return from one to another until they are prepared to meet the everlasting Creator of our entire Universe, of which our solar system is only a very small part . . . for it is self, and selfishness, that would damn the individual soul unto one or the other of those forces that bring about the change that must be in those that willfully wrong [their] Maker . . . It is that which is done, or left undone, or that indifference toward the creation that makes or loses for the individual entity. Then let's be up and doing — doing.   3744-3

31

Finally, to summarize Saturn's function of remolding or reclamation, the following reading compares Saturn with the earth:

For the earth and Saturn are opposites, as it were; for to Saturn goes those that would renew or begin again, or who have blotted from their experience much that may be set in motion again through other influences and environs that have been a portion of the entity's experience.   945-1

The sex glands are associated with Saturn, according to the readings.

URANUS

There is less variation between astrology textbooks and the readings in the meaning of Uranus.

One of the astrology magazines says that Uranus is concerned with occultism, originality, altruism, change, independence; the metal, uranium; the ankles, as part of the body; and ruler of the sign Aquarius.

McCaffery says: "Uranus is peculiarly the planet of insight into the laws of nature. This insight seems to come in flashes, which reveal just how and when material things can be made more useful. It is the planet of the inventor, and is original and scientific, almost never emotional . . . Uranus is the planet of electricity. It is sometimes said to be malefic, for when it strikes, it can cause the whole efforts of a lifetime to tumble down and be destroyed. This is usually because the plan of life has been wrong. The old has to be destroyed before something new can enter . . . It is sometimes said to be the planet of revolutionaries, for it is never content to allow old institutions to continue without change. For this reason Saturn and Uranus are ever in mortal conflict."

The key word for the meaning of Uranus, in the readings, is *extremes,* as the reader will have noted from allusions to it in the Saturn section. It is also the planet of occultism, as distinct from psychic, which means "of the soul, spiritual," according to the readings. Textbooks state that Uranus is very likely the higher octave of Mercury, just as Neptune is the higher octave of Venus. The readings state that Uranus, in man's glandular system, refers to the thyroid, the will. Textbooks and the readings are not too far apart in their understanding of Uranus; but as usual the readings seem to add a deeper meaning to the concept of Uranus' role.

Here are some extracts, culled from dozens, on Uranus' extremism:

From the Uranian influences we find the extremist. And these tendencies . . . will develop especially through the early teen-age years, when there will be moods and the tendency for wonderments . . . These [Uranian tendencies]

32

make for also the intuitive influences and the abilities for the development in the very psychic forces of the entity. 1206-3

In the urges from astrological aspects we find Mercury, Uranus, Venus and Jupiter as the influences through which the entity has received an awareness.
One of high mental ability, yet one very extreme in many ways.
Oft the entity is too easily discouraged. Hence . . . it will require that the entity set a purpose and a goal, and be not deterred from same . . . 2572-1

Those of exceptional abilities with Uranian influence may be *well* said also to mean exceptional abilities to err, or to be led astray in the direction not best for self or self's development. 38-1

In Uranus we find the extremes, and the interest in the occult — or the mystical. This is well if it is balanced in the spiritual nature . . . 2571-1

In those as seen in benevolent influences in Mars and Uranus [both in Libra, sign of balance], these bring . . . exceptional abilities as respecting intuitive forces for the body, and . . . to quiet those who would show wrath or any unkindly feeling toward another. Oft will the entity — if trained, especially in the formative period — be able to act as oil upon troubled waters, as that inter-between will make for beauty in the lives of those the entity contacts, making for a bond of sympathy, of union that will be exceptional . . . as well as that which may be trained for an awakening of abilities within self . . . that will bring for one that may be the peacemaker, not only among individuals, but in groups, in classes, in states, in masses. [Entity entered from Jupiter, with Venus, Mars and Uranus also influencing.] 1911-1

This entity, we find, took its flight, or position, from the planet of Uranus, with Venus and Mercury controlling the destiny in the present earth's plane. Hence the necessity of the entity's training, especially in those elements having to do with purity in love and affection, and of nobleness and goodness for the goodness that comes with that mode of expressing itself in earth's plane, for with the entity under these influences, with the exceptional conditions as come from influences of Uranus, we find the entity's manifestations in the present plane will be exceptionally good or very bad. 143-1

[The entity] is not only a Uranian but an Atlantean, and the combination will be something to *deal with!* as to temper, as to having its own way; for it *will* have its way, irrespective, for the first fourteen years . . .
As for the aspects in the Uranian influence, we find the extremes. The entity will be at times very beautiful in character — at other [times] very ugly; very beautiful in body and mind — at [other times] the other extreme. For these will have an influence and the entity will be an extremist through the first fourteen years of its experience.
High mental abilities. One that will make a study of how to have its way . . .
Do not break the will . . . rather, give the lesson by precept and example. 1958-1

In the Uranian influence we will find the extremes . . . For these will be periods, naturally with a Uranian, when for a few hours or a few minutes or a few days, it will be very, very morose . . . These will arise within the experience from out of nowhere . . .   2005-1

Some readers will get a clue, here at least, as to why they may have sudden and extreme moods which seem to descend from nowhere. Uranus is probably one of the planets under whose influence their entry was made into the earth plane. See the last sentence of the previous reading, and also the following:

Astrologically, then: we find the entity coming under the influence of Mercury, Jupiter, Saturn, Venus and Uranus . . .

In that seen in influences in the Uranian, [it] brings for periods when there seems to be every condition imaginable awry — whether business relations, social relations, financial conditions — every condition seems to be awry. Again there are seasons [when] most things come too easy. These are to be met with that of that *builded* in self through the *mental* abilities, and the stableness of purpose as may be builded by self.   5-2

In Uranus we find the extremes. Thus the entity in spiritual, in mental and in material things finds periods when it is as to the mountain tops and again in the depths of despair.   3706-2

The following excerpt indicates that Uranus combined with Mercury accounts for garrulity.

Easily might the entity become one that would talk of self too much.
While the entity will ever be a good listener, do direct the entity so that there is always the consideration for others.

Astrologically — we find Uranus (the extremist, of course, in same), Mercury (the high mental abilities); for at least eight to ten experiences . . .
                                        2922-1

In a reading on the evolution of the soul, we find that after the soul has gone to Saturn for reclamation, the return can be, or perhaps must be, through Uranus. Here are portions of the reading:

. . . can one but know that each thought, each act, is that being builded, [one] can see how, where, what way and manner each — in their sojourns in the spheres — make for this entering in. As in earth — we have that position in which matter takes all its various forms of presentation of a given energy, *or* forces, as radiated from the various effects of this solar aspect, and take on *bodily* form, occupying a position of, as it were, three in one — or all force in *this* sphere taking on that appearance of that known as threefold, or the aspects of a threefold nature. As in Jupiter — taking on those ennobling forces, whether they may be from earth, from Venus, from Mercury, from Mars, they are *broadened*, they are *changed* in their aspects, in their forms, as they are

34

taken on in and about *this* sphere. As in Saturn — that to whom all insufficient matter is cast for its remolding, its changing into the various spheres of its activity, either re-entering through those of the Uranian — which makes for the accentuations of very good or very bad, and making, in their relationships through the activity of *relative* relations throughout the other experiences, for *extraordinary* conditions; taking on those forces known in earth's planes as from occult influences.   311-2

The Law of Balance

When the influences of Saturn and Uranus are part of the planetary urges of an individual, it seems logical to assume that such an individual has a special lesson to learn about applying the spiritual Law of Balance. Torn between the urges to extremes from Uranian sojourns, and the changes constantly presenting themselves, both inwardly and outwardly, from Saturn's influence, the individual would find himself in a constant state of flux. This might force the will to make decisions about balance between the extremes. Several readings seem to be pointing up such a need.

We find in Uranus the extremes, because of an *inner* feeling; and not merely because of the age or of changes wrought in the material environs . . . For, we find periods when apparently without reason outwardly there is the over-enjoyment . . . and then others when [the entity] becomes rather the recluse, or morose, or . . . inclined to "sulk," as called by some. . .

Make thy life . . . the well-rounded life; preparing self for the home rather than for a career. For, the greatest career of *any* individual is to make a home in such a measure or manner that each occupant — yea, each visitor to same — is better for having known and come into contact with the entity.   2443-1

The person for whom the following reading was given entered from Uranus, with six additional planets influencing the mental urges (irrespective of will). One of the six is Neptune, next to be discussed. Yet we find this admonition to keep the balance:

. . . and while the body-mental may be termed the *exceptional* in mental abilities, these should be guided in the proper channels and kept as of a *unit* of whole expression; knowing that to side-track, to accentuate, any one portion of experiences in the mental or physical forces of the body is to prevent the well-rounded development as is necessary for an individual to apply in its mental, moral, physical, and spiritual development in the material plane . . .

Keep thine heart pure, thine body strong, thine mind open. Attune thine inner man to the harps and the chords of the universe, and harken to the love that brings service — service — to all.   1735-2

Uranus in the glandular system is represented by the thyroid, the will.

35

NEPTUNE

Neptune is the sixth planet outward from the earth, counting Earth as number one. We find that the textbooks and readings agree in assigning mysticism and love of the sea to Neptune. Neptune is supposed to be the higher octave of Venus, and is also associated with the arts. One magazine says Neptune symbolizes compassion, the cinema, dreams, esthetic interests, liquor, gases, vapors, odors.

McCaffery states that Neptune, like Venus, rules music; that it gives second sight and the gift of prophecy; it is diffuse, elusive, emotional and mystical. "Neptune makes mystics, whereas Uranus makes occultists . . . Neptune's vibrations can give the composer in one moment the whole of an opera. It will depend upon the rest of the chart whether this will be written in musical score, for Neptune of itself does not contribute any love of active hard work. The Neptunian inclines to be the dreamer."

We cite a few extracts from the readings which illustrate these points:

. . . the soul and spirit took its flight . . . from that far-away force as exercised in Neptune. Hence we have an entity that . . . will be peculiar to other people, rarely ever being understood; yet one with the spiritual insight of the developing in [the] earth plane, and one whom others would be, could be, benefited by, by being in contact with this entity.   2553-8

For the extremes of Uranus as well as Neptune are a portion of the entity's experience . . .

From Neptune we find that being close to waters, on waters, or about waters, is very well . . . and this also gives those abilities as the mystic — the interest in the unusual, as in the abilities of seeing, feeling, experiencing that which to most would be the unseen forces about the entity.

These are well to be cultivated, not abused, not encouraged by giving thought to what the reaction should be, but keep the spiritual import, the spiritual necessity — which has been a portion of the entity's experience through one of its sojourns, as one who accepted the veil.   2308-1

Neptune *and* Uranus make for an interest in reading matter that is of unusual nature. Things that pertain to mysteries, or conditions in individuals' or groups' lives that are unusual, the uncanny and such . . .

And, for the better development of the entity, as it develops or progresses through the experiences of this sojourn, the dwelling near large bodies of water, or upon large bodies of water, will be the natural elements for the development; giving rise to the abilities both in the occult and in the mystic influences. 406-1

The following excerpt indicates that the soul entered from Neptune, with Uranus, Jupiter and Mars influencing through the tendencies:

Hence the conditions as are exhibited in the present earth's plane, in . . . love of the sea (see, the body has gone to sea).

In the influences, then, we find one of many exceptional abilities.

One that is considered eccentric and peculiar, having many changeable moods.

One loving mystery and every condition as regards . . . a mystery of the sea, and of the sleuth or detective nature.

One that should have been guided close in the study of those things pertaining to the mystery and the occult.

One who will find the . . . greatest abilities in the present earth's plane in the study of the occult forces.   2213-1

In Neptune we find the inclination towards things that have to do with water, and over water, and to be on waters . . . These, then, give an urge again, as through Saturn, for change of scene and change of environment — and the desire for travel . . . those things that are exciting . . . that pertain to the heroic and hero worship. This urge must ever be tempered, then, with directing the entity to the character of ideals . . .   1426-1

In the following, the entity entered from Neptune, which in the natal chart is located at 10 Virgo. According to orthodox astrology, a watery planet in an earth sign is more or less at home, although Neptune is positioned in a sign opposite the one it is supposed to rule, Pisces. All this is interesting in view of the reading.

Here we find unusual conditions, especially owing to the long periods of interims between material sojourns. And thus . . . one that oft appears to be lost in confusion of itself, being highly sensitive to those influences from without.

Thus . . . an entity whose psychic abilities — if developed — may surpass much of that which has been the experience of many . . .

Hence the need for the study, the directing, the instructing of the entity in the sources of spiritual (not spiritualistic, but spiritual) influences . . .

In the astrological aspects we find Neptune, Uranus, Venus and Saturn as the greater influence . . . Hence we will find the inclination for seeking the unusual places, strange conditions — taking up with and associating with strange surroundings, having strange playmates — the desire for [the] unusual in pets . . .

From the Neptune influences — keep away from large bodies of water! These are opposite from much of that accredited as an influence from the astrological aspects of Neptune; though those things that come *from* and *over* large bodies of water . . . will be of a great interest to the entity; and the knowledge of same should be a part of the entity's experience.   2005-1

In the case of [4228] (see chart, p. 61), we find an interesting tie-in of Neptune with Arcturus, the greater Sun of our solar system.

Please note that Mars and Septimus are afflicted; both are located in Cancer (if Septimus is Pluto, as we have reason to think). The language given here as to how the soul took its flight to earth is unusual.

We find the soul and spirit entity took its flight, or its force being present and bringing this present entity's completeness, from . . . Venus' forces, with those of Jupiter, Mercury, Neptune being the ones in the assistance to the conditions bringing to forces to this present plane's development, with afflictions in those in Mars and in that of Septimus. Arcturus being in the greater force for this development upon this plane, [the soul] receiving then the greater force by the influence of Arcturus, with . . . the dwelling-forces of Neptune. The Moon's forces being those that have brought, and will bring, many of the influences from the forces of Venus . . .

As these, we find those inclinations:

With the strength of Jupiter forces, with that of Venus and Neptune . . . one given to letters, and of high exalted positions of self and all concerned therewith. Given to make show, or display, of that element that gives the greater expression of self. Hence, will must be directed, else with the influence of Venus' forces [it] would give detrimental elements in the life.

One whose forces from . . . Mercury will turn in the middle portion of life to those elements pertaining to the chemical forces, with that of Arcturus' forces giving strength to the elements [that are] directed in the entity.   4228-1

Neptune, in the body's glandular system, is represented by the cells of Leydig or lyden.

PLUTO

The planet Pluto was discovered in 1930, and even now there is some mystery and disagreement among astrologers in their interpretation of its meaning.

One astrology magazine says Pluto opposes the conservative, and whatever is usual and accustomed. According to this reference, Pluto opposes individualism and all forces tending toward individuals, in favor of mass movements, with their race riots, and governmental tendencies toward socialism.

McCaffery is not so pessimistic. She says, in *Graphic Astrology,* that in most cases "Pluto merely throws people out of routine, so that adjustments have to be made. It is too early in the study of Pluto to list all the matters under its control." She disagrees that Pluto rules dictators, for dictatorship has existed from remote centuries, and Uranus is more dictatorial than Pluto. She suggests that Pluto has some rule over Scorpio, and also has rule over Aries. Research on Pluto is continuing. McCaffery states in another of her books, *Astrology: Its History and Influence in the Western World,** "My own finding is that it rules change — a change that marks the end of an old condition and the beginning of a new. The changes brought about by Pluto, however, are not the sudden dynamic changes such as are brought about by Uranus. In fact they are often unappreciable for a long period, but they are definite ones."

As we have previously mentioned, the readings indicate that Saturn rules changes, and Uranus, extremes. Impulses from either are testing periods for the soul-entity, and can be considered good or bad according to the way in which you view schooling or hard lessons. In this sense, if Pluto means a shifting of routines, and mass movements that negate the individual, Pluto must be considered a "malefic" by orthodox astrological standards.

We prefer the word "regeneration" with reference to Pluto, since it is a higher-octave planet, as are Uranus and Neptune. In this case, *regeneration* means a higher consciousness and closer to the ideal, the Christ Consciousness. There is some evidence for this in the Edgar Cayce readings. But first let us consider the names themselves.

Pluto is the seventh planet outward from the earth, and prior to its discovery in 1930 the readings mentioned a planet *Septimus,* Latin for *seventh.* Later readings mentioned Pluto by name and [826-8] gave the categorical statement that Pluto and the legendary *Vulcan* were one and the same.

Septimus is mentioned more often in the readings than are Pluto and Vulcan. The actual meanings of the urges from Septimus are unclear and fragmentary, and the meanings are usually those of an "afflicted" planet.

Astrologically, we find most all, in varied spheres, reacting through the soul-consciousness of the entity; Mercury, Pluto, Mars, Venus, Jupiter, Saturn, Neptune. All of these in various manners.

Sudden changes are indicated in Saturn; high mental ability and capabilities in Mercury; *self-centeredness* in Pluto, an earthward in the application of self. [Pluto is in Gemini.]

In Venus we find the attraction to and from the opposite sex; in Jupiter a universal consciousness; in Neptune an interest in psychological and spiritual things.

We find in Mars a high, exalted opinion of self; which is well, but abused — as it may be in Pluto, or in Mercury — may become a stumbling stone rather than a stepping stone to advancement in this present sojourn.   3126-1

*Scribners, N.Y., 1942

39

One of the first life readings given by Mr. Cayce (November 16, 1923, seven years before Pluto was discovered and named) mentions Septimus.

In the relation to . . . the planets that [have], that [are] and that will influence this body we find the strongest of these at the moment of the birth . . . Venus and Neptune were the ruling forces for this body, with those of Mars in the 9th house, of Jupiter in the 12th house, of Uranus in the 7th house, see? Septimus: Almost at its zenith, yet not the ruling factor in this body's actions on this present plane, for with the position of Venus and Neptune this, the influence of Septimus, has become changed by the position of Pisces and the constellations of . . . Castor and Apollo . . .

One well gifted towards the arts, especially in that of writing, or of composition, or of imagination, or of that that has to do with the finer things of life, as would be through the position [of] Castor, Apollo, Venus and Neptune. One [who] should be nearer the great waters for its best development . . . will be well for this body to be wary of that of the influence of Septimus and the conjunction that will be within the next six months, else . . . accident either through self or from the conditions of the trunk or the torso of the body . . .   583-1

Venus in the sunrise chart of this entity is placed at 6 Cancer, and within the next six months, or on May 18, Venus would conjoin natal Pluto at 9 Cancer.

In the influences that bring for warnings, as seen in Mars and Vulcan — beware of fire, and especially of firearms, or explosives . . . Beware of wrath in self, and in grudges as may be builded through wrath's influences in the relationships of the fellowman . . . Keep self attuned to the love force, even as in the occult influences. Beware of those . . . forces as make through chance . . . as of cabalistic or paleozoistic influences.   1735-2

Vulcan and the Dog Star (Sirius) are coupled in the following reading, and these are the influences attributed to them:

In astrological associations, these would appear adverse in their first appearance, coming much under the influence of the Dog Star and Vulcan. These make for that influence as has been of sudden changes in the social affairs, the relationships as respecting those of kinship, and those changes as respecting physical or business relations; yet these *adversities* may be used . . . as stepping stones for [the] soul's development, as well as of a mental and material change in the experience of the entity. As has been oft aptly quoted, it doesn't matter so much as to rebuffs as to the manner and the *use* same is put *to* in the experience of an individual . . . for in adversities *most* conditions grow, provided same is not of a nature to break the *will,* or to make for those conditions in which an entity reaches that position wherein it pities or belittles its own responsibilities, or its own individuality in the experiences through which it may pass. 1727-1

Septimus (Vulcan or Pluto) is not mentioned under the birth planets in the next reading, but a great deal of advice is given about the transiting planets. Under such advice comes the following:

. . . those that have to do with the afflictions of the body come under . . . the constellation of the Twins, or of Gemini, and that of the Great Bear. They will have to do with those of the digestion as afflicted by Septimus in those that come at two cycles especially in this entity. In that of February 1924, and in March 29 of same calendar year . . . beware of conditions, and be careful of the diet during those periods. [Pluto is at 3 in this natal chart.] 487-1

The most significant statement about Pluto's influence so far encountered in the readings is the following:

Q-2. Just what are the effects of Pluto, in conjunction with one's ascendant?
A-2. This, as we find, is entirely amiss from what we might call a physical expression – but, as we find indicated, these [influences] are a development that is occurring in the universe, or environs about the earth – Pluto. Not, as some have indicated, that it is gradually being dissipated. It is gradually *growing,* and thus is one of those influences that are to be as a demonstrative activity in the future affairs or developments of man towards the spiritual-minded influences, or those influences outside of himself.
These [individuals] in the present, as might be said, are merely [those] becoming aware of same. Rather, within the next hundred to two hundred years there may be a great deal of influence [of Pluto] upon the ascendancy of man; for it's closest of those to the activities of the earth, to be sure, and is a *developing* influence, and not one already established. 1100-27

What the expression "closest of those to the activities of the earth" means, we can only guess. Coming to closer influence? Most directly influencing man's mind? Most potentially spiritual influence of all the planetary "schools" for learning outside the earth plane?

The evidence that this is so, and that Septimus is Pluto and therefore spiritual consciousness, may be inferred in the following reading, in which the development of the Jesus-soul as the perfect pattern is discussed.

In the developing, then, that the man may be one with the Father, [it is] necessary that the soul pass, with its companion the will, through all the various stages of development, until the will is lost in Him and he becomes one with the Father.
The illustration of this we find in the man called Jesus. This man, as man, makes the will the will of the Father, then becoming one with the Father and the model for man . . .

When the soul reached that development in which it reached earth's plane, it became in the flesh the model, as it had reached through the developments in those spheres, or planets, known in the earth's plane, obtaining then One in All.

> As in Mercury pertaining of Mind.
>
> In Mars of Madness.
>
> In Earth as of Flesh.
>
> In Venus as Love.
>
> In Jupiter as Strength.
>
> In Saturn as the beginning of earthly woes, that to which all insufficient matter is cast for the beginning.
>
> In that of Uranus as of the Psychic.
>
> In that of Neptune as of Mystic.
>
> In Septimus [Pluto?] as of Consciousness.
>
> In Arcturus as of the developing.   900-10

Chapter Five

CUSPS AND THE ZODIAC

The readings place considerable emphasis on those who were born on the cusps, that is, the time when one Zodiacal sign is ending and another beginning. Astrology textbooks simply say that such individuals partake of both signs in their characteristics. In all the readings studied by this writer, in which the individual is said to be born in or on the cusp, no mention is made as to which two signs are waning and increasing. For this reason we discuss the Zodiac later.

We are left with a mystery. Why were not the signs called by name? Another mystery is that many persons born on the cusp were not designated as such. This may be because many other influences were at work, and were similar to cusp-influences.

Clearly, from the readings, a person born at such a time is and can be in a very difficult position.

In entering the present experience, we find the entity is indeed one who may be said to be under the influence of . . . the cusps. While such influences are different, according to the information . . . given by many, we find that those who are near to the rising of one influence and the submerging — as it were — of another, are oft in those experiences where . . . they are in a strait, as it were, as to what should be the activity.   801-1

In entering, astrologically, we find the entity coming under the influence of Uranus, Venus, Jupiter, and the cusps. In this [latter] relation . . . these in the physical life may be altered by the environmental conditions, and are changed by the will *or* directing influences in the present experience . . .

Under Uranus — one exceptional in abilities, whether that of the mental or of physical endurance, or application of either.

Under Venus — one loving in temperament, one that may be controlled by the influences as relate to sentiment, rather than . . . duty . . .

In the influences in Jupiter — these will bring strength and ennobling powers in the influence of the entity.

Through the cusps, or that changeable influence in the variations as are experienced, felt or known as conscious innate feeling — these will always bring that of rebellion to the others [who] would dominate.   220-1

In the above reading, for a child five years old, we have no accurate birth hours; but the solar chart for September 22, 1924, puts the Sun at 29 degrees Virgo; Uranus at 19 Pisces, Venus at 13 Leo, and Jupiter at 13 Sagittarius. No sign of the Zodiac is mentioned as influencing the entity.

The individual next cited was born March 21, 1933; no birth-hour is given. Solar chart puts the Sun at 29 Pisces. Uranus, Mercury and Jupiter are given as influencing planets. There is no mention of the Piscean, or Sun-sign influence.

This entity comes upon the cusps; thus we find at times conflicting emotions with the entity. During the formative period of mental and physical developments, we find that the entity may be easily led.   2411-1

The Piscean influence is mentioned in the reading for [282], born March 18, 1906, but not the Arian influence as might be supposed. The Sun is placed at 26 degrees, 58 Pisces.

In entering astrologically, we find the entity coming near the cusps and under the influence of Pisces − in its latter portion. Hence we will find, while the entity has altered much of that ordinarily termed as astrological, these are innate . . . conditions to be warned [about] concerning . . . the physical body.   282-2

Other "cusp-ers" are:

. . . with the abilities untrained, [one] would bring those opposing forces as found in Saturn and the cusps. For in the cusps is seen, with those influences in the Uranian, that these bring those passions or those unruly conditions that may not be subdued by force, but conquered, guided and led in love. [Born March 17, 1913; Sun at 26 Pisces.]   960-4

From the astrological aspects we find the entity almost *exactly* upon the cusps. Hence we will find two influences, and the entity oft needing, requiring, a consideration by those making the choice of environs for the entity during the early portion of its developments . . . For there has been into this keeping, in these beginnings, entrusted in this experience an entity that may mean as much to the world as the entity meant to, means to, America. [Born June 21, 1936; Sun at 29 Gemini.]   1208-1

In the astrological aspects we find the entity coming very close to the cusps, or changes; yet the more definitely decided influences the astrological aspects may have . . . will be in the inclinations for the entity to take himself so seriously as he develops . . .

As the entity astrologically comes under the influences from the astrological sojourns − rather than the astrological positions − we will find Venus, Mercury, Mars and Uranus as a portion of the entity's experiences . . . [Born February 18, 1938; Sun at 28 Aquarius.]   1647-1

Not considered "cusp-ers," apparently, are: [305-1], whose Sun is at 2 Cancer; [398-1], whose Sun is at 6 Cancer; [559-7], whose Sun is at 28 Taurus; [759-1], whose Sun is at 26 Aquarius; [773-1], whose Sun is at 3 Taurus; [1426-11], whose Sun is at 27 Gemini, [1635-3], whose Sun is at 29 Gemini, and many others. The readings are open to much more research in this area.

The Zodiac

It has already been hinted that the signs of the Zodiac did not play an important role in most life readings. This is at variance with astrology textbooks which enumerate characteristics for each sign, and when an individual is born in Gemini, for instance, proceed to describe Geminians and ascribe characteristics to that individual according to his Sun sign. Even though his ascending degree is in a different sign, the inward characteristics, say the textbooks, conform to Gemini.

One key to this discrepancy, aside from the influences carried over from previous incarnations, may be found in reading [8-1] (born August 11, 1890; Sun at 18 Leo). The information is given that the physical birth took place late in the evening of August 11, and "in the early morn" (presumably, August 12) were "the soul and spirit forces completed."

We mention this in passing, to illustrate the fact that according to the readings physical birth and soul birth were not always simultaneous. The reading then proceeds, not to describe the Sun in the Leo type of individual, but to say that the soul and spirit took their flight from Mercury, with the influence of Venus, Jupiter and Uranus, with negative influences from Mars and Neptune. The next paragraph states:

As to those [influences] of the constellations or of the zodiacal signs in the life of this entity, these are merely the wavering influences in the life, and not those directing forces ever present in the inner soul of this entity. These we find in opposition to much that is at present taught or given in [the] earth plane . . .   **8-1**

An explanation of why the planetary influences and previous lives' influences are all-important at birth is given for [1796], born January 7, 1925. Following the descriptions of heredity and environment in their truest senses, the reading proceeds to put the Zodiac in its proper relationship:

Thus we find this entity — as each entity — is in the present the result of that the entity has applied of creative influences or forces in every phase of its

45

experience. Thus it makes for that called by some karma, by others racial hereditary forces.

And thus environment and hereditary forces (as are accepted) are in their reality the activities of the *mind* of the entity in its choices through the experiences in the material, in the mental, in the spiritual planes . . .

There are then those accredited signs or omens or indications of characteristics in the innate and manifested activities of the entity. But these are irrespective of what the entity is to do or will do, respecting same.

In the interpreting of the records here, then, we find the entity from the astrological aspects is influenced not because of the position of the sun, the moon or of the earth in its relationships to planets or zodiacal signs or other influences. Yet all of these are recognized as part of the entity's environment.

1796-1

This entity's Sun is at 16 Capricorn. He is influenced by five planets, beginning with Mercury. He is influenced both by astrological and material sojourns, he was told. Although some people are influenced more by astrological or by material sojourns, a larger percentage are influenced by a combination of the two.

To re-state the above, as put in another reading:

Astrologically, then, we find the influences are not merely because of the position of a star or planet, sun or moon, or any of the astrological aspects or effects or influences; but rather through the entity's activities these have an innate balance because of sojourns and activities of the innate or soul-self through such environs . . .

The material sojourns find expression more in the emotional portion of the entity's being . . .

But from the astrological we find the influences innate, and some are to be cultivated, that may grow, that may expand, and become more a portion of the influence; just as others are to be curbed and a lesson gained and applied rather than allowing self to drift . . .   1700-1

For an individual who was born March 18, with the Sun at 28 degrees of Pisces, but not designated as a "cusp-er," we find a statement which certainly does not clarify the importance of Zodiacal signs.

Hence the entity was born into the earth under what signs? Pisces, ye say. Yet astrologically from the records, these are some two signs off in thy reckoning.   5755-1

This discrepancy may be due to the precession of the equinoxes, which is explained by Ellen McCaffery in *Graphic Astrology:* "The vernal equinox is the day in spring (about March 21) when day and night are equal in time. Astrologically, the equinox falls on the

46

day when the Sun reaches the zero degree Aries. Our signs are thus calculated from what is termed by astrologers the Aries ingress, which . . . is now in the constellation Pisces, or one sign behind."

About 2,000 B.C. the signs and the constellations coincided, and March 21, or the vernal equinox, lay in the sign of the Ram, or Aries. Now the signs and constellations are almost one sign apart.

One almanac says that the chart of the Zodiac showing the human body surrounded by the symbols of the Zodiac was first published about the year 1300. However, as years passed, the Zodiac moved slowly backward along the path of the Sun, and the distance covered up to the present time is close to thirty degrees. This means that the sign of Aries now contains the constellation Pisces; the sign Taurus now contains the constellation Aries, etc. Astronomical observers, the almanac says, use the constellations. This can readily be interpreted from the signs by going backward one symbol.

Astronomers generally agree that it takes 26,000 years, approximately, for the Sun and its family of planets to revolve around the central Sun, Arcturus. This backward revolution is called the precession of the equinoxes. Thus, in 2,100 years, the backward movement puts the vernal equinox one sign behind.

Astronomers do not agree as to what degree of the sign of Pisces is now occupied by the Sun at the vernal equinox: 9 degrees is suggested by one, and 3 degrees by another, etc. At any rate, we are nearing the beginning degrees of the Piscean constellation and thus getting closer to the later degrees of the sign of Aquarius. It is conceded that Jesus of Nazareth lived and carried on His ministry in the early Piscean Age.

It is easy to see, then, that the statement about two signs off (for the March 18 individual) is partially explained. According to hints and statements in the Cayce life readings, as this writer interprets them, the error of an additional sign off may be explained by erroneous adjustments of calendars. The Persian calendar and the Zodiacal signs are supposed to be the most accurate.

In life reading 2011-3, the entity was very much interested in astrology, and was told that this stemmed from an experience in Egypt.

. . . the entity was put in command of the preparations for the associations in the land of Saad and the Golden City, and the Mongoloid land. For to these three the entity was sent to act as an interpreter of the various astrological conditions that were to be drawn [up] by the various groups . . . The interests of the entity in those pertaining to astrology arise from that sojourn; also [things] pertaining to buildings, geometrical signs, symbols, pictures, things

47

that illustrate . . . For the Egyptian and the Persian records are quite varied [at variance]. If the entity would study astrology, do not put the signs in the Egyptian calendar but in the Persian, for the Persian interpretations are more proficient than the Egyptian. This is not belittling the efforts of the entity nor of the Egyptians in those periods, but the variations in time have been corrected by the Persians and not by the Egyptians. The Egyptian calculations are thirty degrees off [one sign].   2011-3

Although we have a possible explanation for the second of the "two signs off," it would take an expert in the subject of ancient calendars with all their discrepancies to explain what this means in terms of the Sun in the Zodiac, in the present.

There are other references in the readings to the Persian calendar. One of these is from 826-8, and we include part of the reading leading up to this because it discusses the matter of which chart should be used for an individual — the physical birth or the soul birth.

Q-5. Should an astrological horoscope be based on the time of physical birth or the time of soul birth?

A-5. On time of physical birth; for these are merely *inclinations*, and because of inclinations are not the influence of will. *WILL* is that factor of the spiritual forces or the gift, as it were, *to* man . . . as he came into material form, with which choice is made, see? Hence if astrological aspects are to be assumed, then physical. But these make for oft confusing experiences to those casting such charts and reading from that which has been the version [interpretation] of same.

For as we have indicated, there are two, yea, three phases or schools through which such information, such charts, such characters have been carried — the Egyptian, the Persian, the Indian.

The Persian is a combination and the *older* of all of these, and these are as logos [?], or as charts that have been set. That they have become as experiences in the activities of individuals, to be sure, is not disputed; but the world does not govern *man*, MAN governs the world! And the inclinations astrologically show whether man has or has not applied will!

Then the inclinations are good, but they may be stumbling stones if one submerges will to listen at inclinations!   826-8

A reference to our misinterpretation of the Zodiac and to the precession of the equinoxes comes in reading 311-2. This whole reading is worth study, for it touches upon so many puzzling subjects.

. . . the *solar* system is also passing through its various spheres, that are being acted upon by the forces *from* without, or that as is ordinarily known — or has been *determined* and named, though not rightly, or wholly rightly in their aspects — as those forms in the various *months* . . . yet we find a similarity of expression, rather than action. *Action* from the *motive* forces *from* the entity's *experience* or development, or through either the *earth's* experience or the spheres about same. 311-2

The whole purpose of each life reading given by Mr. Cayce was to be helpful to the individual.

In giving that which may be helpful to this entity in the present experience, respecting the sojourns in the earth, it is well that the planetary or astrological aspects also be given. It should be understood, then, that the sojourning of the soul in that environ [planetary], rather than the position [square, trine, etc., or planets at birth], makes for the greater influence in the experience of an entity or body, in any given plane. This is not . . . belittling that which has been the study of the ancients, but rather it is giving the *understanding* of same. And, as we have indicated, it is not so much that an entity is influenced because the Moon is in Aquarius or the Sun in Capricorn or Venus or Mercury in that or the other house, sign, or the Moon and Sun sign, in that one of the planets is in this or that position in the heavens; but rather because those positions in the heavens are from the *entity* having been in that sojourn as a soul! This is how the planets have the greater influence in the earth upon the entity, see? For the application of an experience is what makes for the development of a body, a mind, *or* a soul. 630-2

In summary, the writer believes that the constellations, as well as Zodiacal signs, are important in interpretations of astrological charts. The life readings are replete with references to Arcturus, the Greater Sun, and the way out of this particular solar system, along with Septimus; with references to the Pleiades, Dog Star, Orion, the Great Bear, Polaris and others.

It should not be concluded that the life readings never include descriptions of the signs of the Zodiac. The allusions are simply infrequent and seemingly of secondary importance. Here are a few which have been found.

For [2668], born March 11, 1920, with the Sun at 20 Pisces, no time of the day was given. A solar chart, putting the Sun on the Ascendant as if at sunrise, also puts Uranus at 2 Pisces. This is the only mention of Pisces in the reading:

In entering, we find astrologically the entity coming under the influences in Pisces, in Venus, in Mercury, Jupiter and Uranus. 2668-1

In 276-2, again we have no accurate birth time, and only that the entity was born January 15, 1918. A solar chart shows nothing occupying the sign of Aries, yet the reading states:

In entering, we find the influences astrologically in Aries — which will require in the present experience the use of the mental abilities of the entity in making its choice. Hence . . . through the formative period of the mental developments being especially susceptible . . .   276-2

On August 26, 1913, [641] was born, and the solar chart puts his Sun at 2 Virgo. The sign of Virgo is otherwise unoccupied. The reading states:

In the present experience we find more of those conditions as latent urges than those as have been manifested or expressed through the application of will . . .

In entering the earth's plane, we find the entity coming under the influence of Jupiter, Mercury, Venus and the benevolent influences in [the] Sun and in Orion.   641-1

The three stars in Orion are Betelgeuse at 27 Gemini; Bellatrix at 19.50 Gemini; and Rigel at 15 Gemini. This individual has Mars, Saturn and Pluto in Gemini but none of the three is mentioned as influential planets.

We have both Pisces and Leo mentioned in 2905-3, for which we have only a solar chart. The Moon is in Leo, but is not mentioned as influential; Mercury is in Pisces but is mentioned fourth in importance.

Astrologically we find urges, not because the Moon or the Sun or Leo or Pisces may have been in this or that position when the entity was born. But the entity as a consciousness experienced those activities or awarenesses in those environs. Thus these become part of the soul experience. As will be found, Leo — or the consciousness of that mind — will be a part of the entity's awareness. Thus at times the entity will appear headstrong, willful . . .   2905-3

Again, in a solar chart for [406], born January 16, 1919, the four important planets are Mars, Uranus, Jupiter and Neptune. The reading states:

Through Aries associations, there are the abilities of a high *mental* development; yet there are rather those warnings for this entity regarding accidents to the head. Injuries of some nature may come . . . either during the next four months or early portion of 1934. These warnings are from influences that come from Aries or head associations with Mars.

Hence, as to the greater astrological activities from sojourns in enviorns, Uranus is the greater influence for the present experience.   406-1

No planet occupies the sign of Aries, although Aries may be the ascendant in a correct birth chart, with the time of day known. Mars itself is at 21 Aquarius.

We have a correct birth chart for [1710], born February 26, 1915, near Norfolk, at 6 P.M. (5:56 P.M. local time: 11:00 P.M. Greenwich mean time). Piscean influence is described (Sun is in Pisces) and also the influence of Libra, for which we can find no reason unless Venus, the first planet mentioned, carries the Libran influence. Mercury and Uranus are the other two planets mentioned. Note the positions of Venus, Mercury and Uranus, none of which are "rising" or near the Zenith or Ascendant. (See Figure 6, p. 68.)

We quote significant excerpts from this reading:

There have been periods when the entity apparently has been blocked in the preparation for this or that activity, this or that association with individuals, and circumstances that would have changed or do change the whole course of events for the entity.

These influences all come from the Atlantean's activities that have brought Libra (of the balance) into force in such a manner that it might be said of the entity, indeed there is a path cut out for thee — the gods have directed that ye will have the opportunity to show forth thy worth . . .

In the astrological aspects we find the Piscean influences.

Hence we find the entity apparently oft bearing the brunt of others' misapplication of time or of purpose, or even of material things. But know that such only offers an opportunity for self for greater development in every phase of the experience. Not that these are to always be, but they are as examples of the fact that whom the Lord loveth He *calleth,* and *prepareth* through chastenings, through trials, through those experiences which will develop one for the activities in which greater successes of every nature may come.

For thy talents being many, much will be — is — required of thee.

Kick not against circumstance, that has apparently at times fraughted thee in thy efforts — whether they have been thy social relationships with those of the opposite sex, or whether in the apparent manner of preparation for activities in chosen fields of service in the material world. But know that these have been and are opportunities for *greater* advancement.

In Venus as combined with Mercury, *and* the activities in Uranus, we find the interests in things mechanical as well as those that require the application of such by the material hands . . .

As to the application of self respecting the astrological forces — these as we find are only urges. As to what one does *with* and about same depends upon choices made.

Hence the needs for each soul, each entity to have a standard, an ideal by which the patterns of the life, or its associations with its fellowman, may be drawn.   1710-3

We cannot recognize the orthodox description of Libra from the above, nor reconcile its influence, unless Libra is on the ascendant and we are at least one sign behind! If we are two signs behind and Scorpio is on the ascendant, then Venus, the most influential planet, is just barely rising.

The above might be said to be a good description of Pisces.

Chapter Six

PLANETS, TRANSITS AND CYCLES

Only occasionally, in the life readings, was the accurate birth time given, corrected or verified. By accurate birth time is meant not just the place, the month, day of the month and year, but the time of the day or night, to the minute. Only with the latter information can a correct horoscope be erected, giving the sign and degree at the Eastern or ascending point, together with the correct North, South and West. Then the cusps of the other houses may be put in position.

With the correct information given in approximately forty-five readings (there may be more, as further indexing and research uncovers them), accurate charts have been erected by three competent astrologers. Two of these were professionals not connected with the A.R.E., and one is a member.

At the beginning of this book it was stated that 150 readings for children formed the chief basis of our intensive study. Here is an interesting breakdown of the number of planets which influenced these youngsters:

In only one reading was just one planet mentioned, the one from which the soul took flight.
In four readings, two planets were given as influential.
In twenty-seven readings, three planets were given.
In fifty-two readings, four planets were given.
In twenty-four readings, five planets were given.
In eight readings, six planets were given.
In four readings, seven planets were given.
In one reading, eight planets were given.

The total of these is 121; leaving twenty-nine children's readings in which only earth lives were influential, or in which readings were for very young babies and descriptions but not names of planets were mentioned, and physical warnings about the babies' health were given. Parents were sometimes advised to seek a life reading for the child later on.

It would appear from the above that most people have from four to six planets influencing their lives, and that among this number is the primary or most important one from which the soul took flight. In the readings, this planet is often mentioned first, and usually tallies with the life just preceding this incarnation; the second planet tallying with the life just preceding that one, etc.

In answer 31 from the 3744 series of readings, it is stated that not all the planets are effective in their influence upon an individual, in the present life. The implication is that the entity has not sojourned in some of them recently enough to affect the present life; or the others are not involved particularly with the present planetary-earthly sojourn. Here is the key statement:

The influence from any [planet] is from what planet that soul and spirit returns to bring the force to the earth individual, as it is breathed into the body, from whence did it come, that being the influence? Not the revolution of the ideas as given from those who study of those forces . . .   3744-3

Later on in this same reading, it was asked if the tendencies of an individual are most influenced by the planets nearest the earth at the time of birth. The answer was that the individual is influenced most by the planet at, or close to, the Zenith when the individual soul took its flight in coming to the earth plane. And the Zenith, according to textbooks, is the Midheaven or southernmost point of the circle, farthest away from the person viewing the circle.

We have another clue to the primary planet in the following reading:

The strongest power in the destiny of man is the Sun, first; then the closer planets, or those that are coming in ascendancy at the time of the birth; but let it be understood here, no action of any planet or any of the phases of the Sun, Moon, or any of the heavenly bodies surpass the rule of Man's individual will power – the power given by the Creator of man in the beginning, when he became a living soul, with the power of choosing for himself.

The *inclination* of man is ruled by the planets under which he is born. [To this extent] the destiny of man lies within the sphere of scope of the planets. With the given position of the Solar system at the time of the birth of an individual, it can be worked out – that is, the inclinations and actions [can be worked out] without will power taken into consideration.   254-2

The phrase "coming to ascendancy" means the three houses just below the Ascendant, and the two houses just in front of the Zenith, or Midheaven. At least, these meanings for Zenith and ascending are the ones used in astrology textbooks – how can we be sure the readings used the terms with the same meanings? We cannot.

53

Incidentally, astrology textbooks ascribe great importance to the Ascendant, the Zenith, and planets "rising" or on the left-hand side of the circle. The textbooks try to arrive at the most important planet or planets by various means: the ruler of the Sun-sign, the ruler of the rising sign, the planets most "aspected," etc. Orthodox astrology does not say that all planets equally affect the individual or "native"; neither do the Edgar Cayce readings. To this extent there is agreement.

Transits and cycles are important factors in the individual horoscope, as given in the readings. By transits is meant the changes in position of the planets, Sun and Moon from the birth date on. Here we come to the word "aspect," so important in present-day astrologers' interpretation. As far as we can discover, these are the same as those defined in the textbooks: conjunction, square, opposition, trine, etc. If four planets are given as the influential ones in the reading, with Venus the one from which the soul took flight to earth, for instance; any transiting aspect made by any planet to the natal four, or involving any of the natal four by their present positions, affect the individual.

If, for example, Saturn is not one of the natal four, but is presently squaring Venus, the birth planet, either in the heavens or squaring the natal position of Venus, then Venus will feel the effects of Saturn, the change-about-er! Whatever Venus means in the natal chart, whether it is the love nature or an artistic talent, a changeover may be due. Since all changeovers may be somewhat painful or unsettling, the native, or individual, may feel frustrated and at sea.

On the subject of aspects, as such, it came as a considerable shock to this writer to discover that the natal planets are seldom, or rarely in aspect to each other! If they are, it seems almost accidental; and of all the aspects, we have found that the conjunction is most often found. In the natal chart, two planets may be conjunct, within one to four degrees, and only one of the two be named as one of the influential planets.

As to cycles and their influence upon the individual, the readings indicate that approximately every seven years there is a change and another cycle. There is some evidence that seven years is not allotted to each of the eight planets, that only the (say) four planets mentioned as influential have seven years apiece and at the end of the four cycles the first planet takes the fifth cycle, the second planet the sixth, etc. This of course varies from what is taught in traditional astrology.

As to the appearances of the entity in the earth, and those influences that will bear upon the early experiences — we find that these, as may be seen,

54

should be changed in the seventh and in the fourteenth year. These are as cycles of impressions and changes; and activities in the developing of the body, the mind, the soul ... [Born 12-8-38, at Detroit, Michigan, at 10:47 P.M.]   1788-3

It will be seen, as we find from the records here, that varied experiences of the entity in its developments through the [whole] cycle of its experience will be altered by the variation in the cycles of development; and that as may be given in the present as having the greater influence will during its seventh to fourteenth or fifteenth year be changed — as when it is 21 and 28; and then [at 28] it will be determined as to whether it is to be the material or the mental and spiritual success to which this entity may make for its experiences in the present sojourn. [Born 8-31-36; no planets given]   1332-1

As to the appearances in the earth, not all of these may be given. For these ye attain in thy varied cycles of unfoldment. [Born 2-19-32; no planets given]
3053-3

As there was in the entering of the entity's inner forces into this physical body, the first [change] will come at the age of 7, then at 14, at 22 — these will be decided changes, or one will so lap over the other — but may be said to be periods when changes will come to this entity; for there was some lapse of time (as time is counted from the material) between the physical birth and the spiritual birth.   566-1

As to the appearances in the earth, these have been quite varied. Not all may be given in the present, for with each cycle there comes another experience as a part of the entity's problems or help. Just as some set that each day or each hour, as the earth passes from phase to phase of the *constellations,* or the signs of the zodiac, there comes greater impression. *Rather* is it as [the influence of] the cycles. For it is admitted that the body changes completely each seven years.   3637-1

We have in reading 405-1 a reference to the "second cycle of Jupiter's influence, which begins in 1940." This child of eleven years of age was born March 2, 1922. She entered from Jupiter, according to the reading, with "Mercury and Venus, with Mars" as influential planets. The reading makes it clear that Jupiter affects the whole sojourn and is emphasized by cycles: "Then Jupiter being the ruling influence . . . from the astrological aspects, as the time of birth, as well as to the sojourn of the entity."

Doing a little figuring, it can be seen that from 1922, the birth year, to 1940, the time of Jupiter's second cycle, there is a span of eighteen years. Up to seven years of age, the child was under a Mercury-Jupiter influence; up to fourteen years, under a Venus-Jupiter cycle, ending in 1932 or 1933. Then from fourteen to twenty-one years of age, came a cycle of Mars-Jupiter, which brings us to 1939 or 1940, when the reading states that Jupiter's second cycle begins. This is a piece of evidence that the cycles make the rounds of the influential planets, over and over again.

A Different Kind of Cycle

The quotation from this reading speaks for itself:

... we find in this particular entity, *and oft*, ones that enter an experience as a *complete cycle;* that is, upon the same period under the same astrological experience as in the sojourn just before (that is, being born upon the same day of the month — though time may have been altered); find periods of activity that will be very much the same as those manifested in the previous sojourn, in the unfoldment and in the urges latent and manifested.

Psychology, philosophy, reasoning, dramatic art, the dramatic critic — these will be the character and the temperament that [are] to be dealt with [in this entity.]

For, in the appearance before this, the entity entered as Jean Poquelin, known as Molière, the great French dramatist.   2814-1

Molière was born January 15, 1622. This individual was born January 15, 1942.

We have a few other examples of such cycles. This person was born on October 2, 1940, and the reading stated:

Nickname the entity Franz . . . and there will be seen why . . .

Before this, the entity was in the Austrian or Hungarian land. There the entity was an unusual individual, in the name Liszt; being a composer as well as a musician. And as its activities through the experience were such as to make for certain characters of music, these in part will be of special interest to the entity in the present. The comparison may be easily seen . . . as to the faults, the failures, as well as the activities in which the entity then . . . rose to its place or position in the musical world.

That is why, then, the nickname Franz is suggested; for the entity was Franz Liszt.   2584-1

No accurate birth time was given, and there was no mention of planets. Musician Franz Liszt was born on October 22, 1811.

Patrick Henry was born on May 29, 1736; and this man, whose birth date was May 27, 1940, was described as Patrick Henry in the life just prior. We have the accurate birth time for [2294], as well as planets. He entered from Saturn.

From the astrological aspects we find the influences indicating the energetic activity of the mind as well as of the body.

Also there are the tendencies for extravagance, which should be curbed . . . through the early periods of its activity; for these will be a part of the inclinations, not only because of the Gemini influence, but also the Saturn, Mercury, Jupiter, Mars and Venus influences.

As these planets were strong influences in the earth through the developing periods of . . . gestation, they will in the early portion of the life manifest the greater influence.

Hence we find one that will . . . show a general energetic activity . . . Not that there will not be affection, not that there will not be . . . preferences; but the very nature of the Gemini influence makes for the sudden changes of preferences, and the demonstrations in which there will be seen the influences of these . . .   2294-1

The birth chart for [2294] is on page 62. Beside each planet in the chart, we have indicated the order of mention, putting Saturn first, of course, as in the reading. The reading continued that the entity would have the ability to argue out everything; hence there should always be given the reason *why,* in its training.

As an orator the entity may be found to excel, as in its former experience; but this . . . will necessitate . . . training in those directions. For, as the awareness arises . . . we will find the entity inclined to shut self away at times, and at others to be *over*-active in giving expressions . . . For, in the developing years, there will be the tendency to seek liberty for its own self at any cost; and there should be given the whys, the causes and the expression of the abilities that are reached through the Mercurian high mental experience as well as the benevolent influences through the Uranian sojourn — so as to bring more and more the abilities to express for the universality of the activities . . . Hence the entity should be trained in *International Law* . . .   2294-1

Notice from this chart that the Number One planet, Saturn, is not the one closest to the Zenith, or Midheaven; nor to the Ascendant. All the influential planets are on the left-hand side of the chart, or the rising side, or coming to ascendancy. The 12th house (just above the Ascendant) is generally ignored as an important rising house by astrologers; yet in this chart, Mercury, the second most important planet is just above the Ascendant, in the 12th house.

This person, [2294], is not described as a Sun-in-Gemini type of person; however, Gemini influences him, presumably because Mercury (ruler of Gemini) is in Gemini and very close to the Ascendant. Also presumably, the life just before this was ruled by Mercury primarily, and the reading says this was a "Mercurian high mental experience." This could of course mean in the environs of Mercury also. We do know that progress, or soul-evolution, is made by application of lessons learned in planetary sojourns to the problems of earth life.

Summary

The text of this booklet contains only a small portion of the 2,500 life readings that Edgar Cayce gave during his lifetime. To date, neither the author nor others have attempted a complete survey of all the astrological references in the A.R.E. Library. What pertinent items still lie uncovered is a matter of deep interest to many of those concerned with Astrology and the continuing work of the Association. Certainly a vast amount of material is available for further research and interpretation.

In closing, let the following reading (given 2-14-24) continue the theme of universal soul forces, with planetary influences playing their usual accompanying role:

Q-39. What are the laws governing relativity of all force?

A-39. In giving the manifestation of such a law, which does exist, we first must consider that that is called force, and that force then in its relation, or the relativity of that force to all force.

There are, as were set in the beginning, as far as the concern is of this physical earth plane, those rules or laws in the relative force of those that govern the earth, and the beings of the earth plane, and also that same law governs the planets, stars, constellations, groups, that that constitutes the sphere, the space, in which the planet moves. These are of the one forces, and we see the manifestation of the relation of one force with another in the many various phases as is shown, for in fact that which to the human mind exists, in fact does not exist, for it has been in past before it is to the human mind in existence.

In this, we see the law of the relations of conditions, space or time and its relation to human mind, as is capable of obtaining information upon the earth plane from a normal force or conditions. Hence, we bring the same word, relativity of force, to prove its own self, and condition, for we have as in this:

The earth in its motion, held in space by that force of attraction, or detraction, or gravitation, or lack of gravitation in its force, so those things that do appear to have reality, and their reality to the human mind, have in reality passed into past conditions before they have reached the mind, for with the earth's laws, and its relations to other spheres, has to man become a past condition. So it is reached only in the further forces as will show, and as is

58

given, for man to understand in this developing, or this evolution from sphere to sphere, or from plane to plane, in this condition.

Hence, we find to the normal mind, there is no law as to relativity of force, save as the individual may apply same in the individual's needs of them. That is sufficient.

Then in a later paragraph the reading offered further insight and guidance to gaining of awareness in relationship with these universal forces.

The study from the human standpoint, of subconscious, subliminal, psychic, soul forces, is and should be the great study for the human family, for through self man will understand its Maker when it understands its relation to its Maker, and it will only understand that through itself, and that understanding is the knowledge as is given here in this state.   3744-4

Birth Charts and Examples of Life Readings

FIGURE 1
(see p. 37)

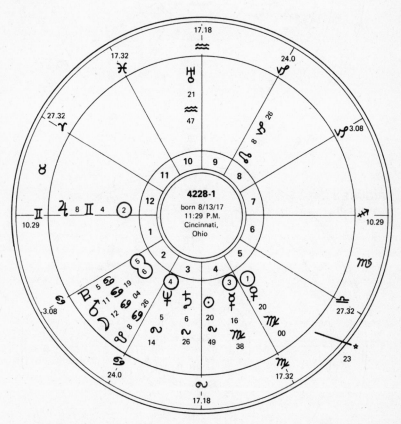

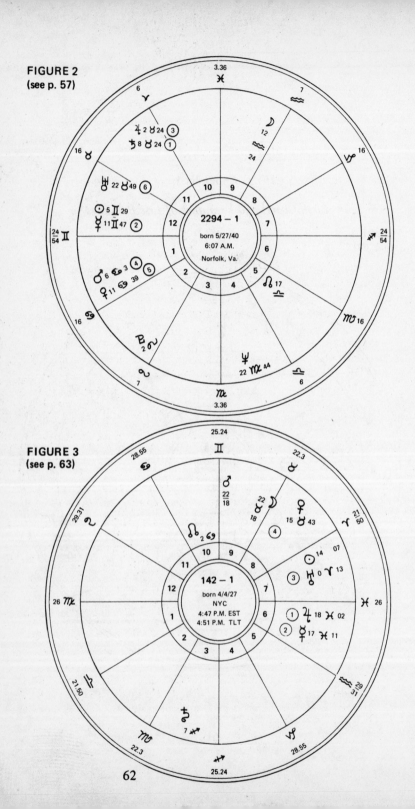

FIGURE 2
(see p. 57)

2294 – 1
born 5/27/40
6:07 A.M.
Norfolk, Va.

FIGURE 3
(see p. 63)

142 – 1
born 4/4/27
NYC
4:47 P.M. EST
4:51 P.M. TLT

Example to Figure 3   Given 5-15-27

142-1   Male, 1 mo.   Born 4-4-27

(This is of special interest in light of warnings given about firearms, for an individual indicated to have been previously killed in a duel.)

In entering, we find the entity comes under the influence of Jupiter and Mercury with benevolent influences in Uranus and in Venus; hence we will find there will be many unusual conditions which will surround those influences as will be exhibited in the life of the entity. Yet as we find, there is also presented, through those cosmic influences and through the astrological conditions, those of the warnings as would be presented for the development of the mental, the physical and the spiritual influences as will become manifested through urges as will be exhibited in this body. Principally these have to do with those conditions regarding temper and the exercising of same as regards the will's influence. Not, then, that the will of the entity shall be broken but that same shall be guided in those directions that will bring the more benevolent and more powerful influence in the life through the Jupiterian influence.

Again we find that there will appear the square of those conditions between Mars and Uranus with Jupiter in the twelfth year in which the warning is especially against the relations of the entity as regarding firearms . . .

There appears, as we see, the greater influence in Jupiter and in Mercury, with the benevolent influence in Uranus which becomes as exceptional conditions in the urges; being then very decided in the likes and dislikes, being inclined toward those conditions and positions of estate and of high mental and physical influence; inclined then toward aspiring to same through the abilities of the mental.

Hence the injunction as is given toward the direction of the will's influence in the life as respecting control of temper. For in this there may be brought those detrimental conditions especially as regarding the misapplication of station or position, rather than inclined towards those not of the plebian but of those in the position of the leader. For the natural intent of the entity is toward that of the natural leader in the mental, in the social, in the political, in the financial forces of those who surround the entity.

63

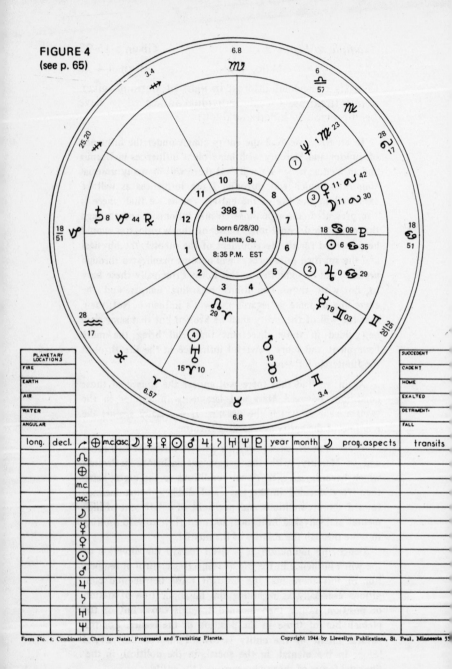

FIGURE 4
(see p. 65)

398 – 1
born 6/28/30
Atlanta, Ga.
8:35 P.M. EST

PLANETARY LOCATIONS				
FIRE			SUCCEDENT	
EARTH			CADENT	
AIR			HOME	
WATER			EXALTED	
ANGULAR			DETRIMENT.	
			FALL	

long.	decl.	♐	⊕	m.c.	asc.	☽	☿	♀	☉	♂	♃	♄	♅	♆	♇	year	month	☽	prog. aspects	transits
		♌																		
		⊕																		
		m.c.																		
		asc.																		
		☽																		
		☿																		
		♀																		
		☉																		
		♂																		
		♃																		
		♄																		
		♅																		
		♆																		

Form No. 4; Combination Chart for Natal, Progressed and Transiting Planets.   Copyright 1944 by Llewellyn Publications, St. Paul, Minnesota 55

64

Example to Figure 4   Given 3-31-33
398-1   Female, 3 yrs.   Born 6-28-30
(For a child whose mother, a professional astrologer,
saw in the child's chart danger of death in early
childhood.)

In entering from the astrological and astronomical viewpoint
. . . these would at some periods be very much in line with
that ordinarily attributed to such — in *some* ways of judging
same; while others are in almost opposition to that ordinarily
adjudged as the astrological influence.

Coming under the influence of Neptune then, as we find,
makes for the mystic forces in the experience of the entity;
as liking and loving a mystery . . . So, one that has encompassed
or covered the greater period in the developing of the
individual entity or soul would be called the old, or the more
highly evolved, or greater developed soul. This one will be
unusual!

In the approaching of both Jupiter and Venus in their
conjunction with the attributes of the triad [trine?], or the
angle at which same comes to Uranus through the birth
period of the entity . . . we find these not as the *influencing*
in the experience of the entity, but as the relationships of
those sojourns or planetary influences upon the dwellers upon
the earth during this particular period they *influence* the life
of the entity *by* their contributing to the impelling influences
in the entity's experience . . .

So, with the directing through the period [of youth], know
that these conditions arise from those influences that make for a
strong, well, healthy physical body, and that the attributes
are such that these may be led in that which becomes
excessive in the forces of the mental only, or the spiritual-
mental, or the carnal forces. As to these, those that direct
must choose; hence the responsibility that comes upon those
that would guide or direct.

With the tendencies in those influences from the sojourns
. . . there comes those tendencies also wherein, unless these
are developed into those channels where they come from the
spiritual or the creative forces of the developing influences for
the entity, not to be deceitful so much — but rather as one
with the ability to *tweedle* [wheedle] . . . this, that or the
other out of whatever source or channel it would try or
attempt to do; and what is the life of a [wheedler]!

65

Yes, we have the body, [398], and those conditions in the astrological aspects; especially in reference to those adverse influences that appear eminent in the experience of the entity in the near future; as well as that which has been built by the entity in its sojourns through the spheres of activity where there is such a gathering of influences as to become active in a body-entity.

In giving that which may be understandable, and that which may be helpful from the material angle at this time, as we find, it would be well that all consider the varying aspects from that considered an astrological influence.

As we have given through these channels, astrological influences are effective in the experience of each and every entity. However, when the activities of a soul-entity have been such as to cause or to form the appearance of the entity in a particular sphere of [planet] activity, the position of the sojourn of the entity *to* the earth *has* the greater influence than just the adverse or benevolent positions of the planet or of a whole solar system upon the *entity's* activity! . . .

Then, it is as this: When the activities of an entity, a soul in the earth, have been such that its passage from the earth would become a birth into the realm of matter known as Mars, Venus, Jupiter, Uranus, Neptune, Moon, Mercury, Polaris, or any of these that are effective in the universal influence, you see, the sojourn there *and* the position of the planets *are* more effective than the influence brought to bear because of a position in a certain place or portion of the universal forces, see?

Hence, as we find, these conditions are only as urges; or, as may be termed from some reasons or seasons of thought, the planetary influences from their positions are either benevolent, adverse or inter-between these activities — one drawing upon another; but the entity's *sojourn* IN those environs makes the impulse for the mental activity, rather than the *position* of these!

Do we gather the variation?

Hence, for this particular entity at this time, as we find, there will be those conditions in which there will be seen adverse influences in the activity of the entity as related to the material sojourn of the body; but these will be rather in the form of *mental* DEMONSTRATIONS within the activity of the body, than purely mechanical-physical or physical-mechanical — whichever you would choose to term it!

Then, they will be *impulses* — and may be seen in the entity's experience particularly through this period, beginning with the fifth (5th) of September to the eighth or tenth (8th or 10th) of October, this present year.

As to what is to be done respecting such conditions, it would be well that all precautions known in the activity of the earth be taken (as particular attention to the activities of the body, and the hygienic influences in the experiences of the body) to avert an adverse influence in the health of the body itself. See?

Why? The question may be asked, why the mental hygiene, why the physical hygiene, particularly?

Because of those influences of the mental nature that would cause the body to be attracted to the character of influences that would be detrimental to the physical welfare or sojourn in the earth during that particular period!

It would be the same way that one might feel (this aside, of course) within self when awakening from a sleep, or from a revery, or from some mental urge to do or see or know something pertaining to something that apparently has nothing to do with the activities of the body-physical; as the mental desires to know of certain forces, forms, elements, or activities of elements, at that particular or immediate time. See?

Hence the same is active in this particular experience at this time of this body we are speaking of . . .

67

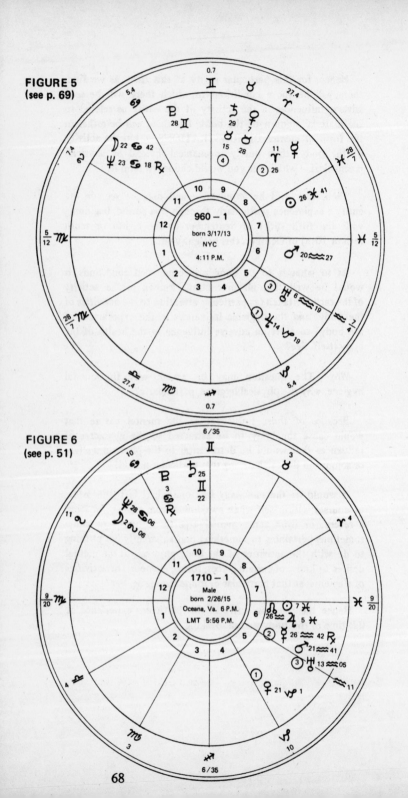

FIGURE 5
(see p. 69)

(see p. 69)

960 – 1
born 3/17/13
NYC
4:11 P.M.

FIGURE 6
(see p. 51)

(see p. 51)

1710 – 1
Male
born 2/26/15
Oceana, Va. 6 P.M.
LMT 5:56 P.M.

Example to Figure 5   Given 12-2-27

960-4   Male, 14 yrs.   Born 3-17-13

(This reading, for a boy born deaf, indicated he had been involved in the French Revolution.)

This body is under the influences of Jupiter, Mercury, and Uranus with those afflictions in Saturn. As to these influences as are seen, irrespective of the application of will's forces we find:

The inability of the entity to understand why that ego should be subjugated to another. Hence with these complicating conditions in the present plane, we find much care, much attention should be given in that stage when the mind and the reactions from same will give that correct balance with same, that the entity may develop toward that oneness of purpose.

In the universal forces found in the astrological conditions and positions, irrespective of the will, we find one that has innate high and noble purposes. He is often misunderstood, and when rebuked, the entity little understands why . . .

One that is high-tempered, yet, guided in the correct way and manner, will bring much joy, much happiness, much of better understanding to those that would be found in oppression, and one that would bring release to many.

He should be a lawyer. One that will bring through those abilities, guided aright, those conditions of the more . . . knowledge of that unison, of the purpose in *right for right's sake,* and not because another says this is right or wrong.

One that with the abilities untrained, would bring those opposing forces as found in Saturn and the cusps. For in the cusps is seen, with those influences in the Uranian, that these bring those passions or those unruly conditions that may not be subdued by force, but conquered, guided and led in love. One that when guided aright may make same manifest in many ways, as meted in justice, and as given in literature. For these, as seen, to many, become the thought of this entity.

One that is mindful of conditions and doesn't desire to see anything or anyone suffer. While the idea of tease or taunt is seen at times, most is a direct debt toward those that would persecute another.

Appendix II

Zodiac – Planetary Signs and Symbols

For those readers unfamiliar with the symbols and terminology of traditional astrology, this Appendix and the Glossary following are included. This material has been compiled from standard texts and references, along with explanations from the readings where noted.

TABLE "A"   SIGNS OF THE ZODIAC

	ZODIAC HEMISPHERE (N-S)	SIGN SYMBOL	PROPHET DISCIPLE	RULING PLANET (Body Parts)	MASC. FEM.
I	Aries — (N)	Ram	Malachi	Mars	
	(Mar. 21-Apr. 20)	(Fire)	Mathias (Mark)	(Head & Face)	♂
II	Taurus — (N)	Bull	Haggai	Venus	
	(Apr. 21-May 21)	(Earth)	Thaddeus	(Throat & Neck)	♀
III	Gemini — (N)	Twins	Zachariah	Mercury	
	(May 22-June 21)	(Air)	Simeon-Simon	(Hands, Shoulders Lungs & Nerves)	♂
IV	Cancer — (N)	Crab	Amos	Moon	
	(June 22-July 23)	(Water)	John	(Breast & Stomach)	♀
V	Leo	Lion	Michael-Hosea	Sun	
	(July 24-Aug. 23)	(Fire)	Jacob (James)	(Heart, Sides Upper Back)	♂
VI	Virgo — (N)	Virgin	Isaiah	Mercury	
	(Aug. 24-Sept. 23)	(Earth)	Thomas	(Solar Plexus Bowels)	♀
VII	Libra — (S)	Scale Bearer	Luke	Venus	
	(Sept. 24-Oct. 23)	(Air)		(Kidneys Lower Back)	♂
VIII	Scorpio — (S)	Scorpion	Judas	Pluto	
	(Oct. 24-Nov. 22)	(Water)		(Bladder Sex Organs)	♀
IX	Sagittarius — (S)	The Archer	Zephaniah-St. George	Jupiter	
	(Nov. 23-Dec. 21)	(Fire)	Andrew	(Liver, Blood Hips & Thighs)	♂
X	Capricorn — (S)	Goat	Jonah-Nahum	Saturn	
	(Dec. 22-Jan. 20)	(Earth)	Peter	(Knees-Spleen)	♀
XI	Aquarius — (S)	Water Bearer	Matthew	Uranus	
	(Jan. 21-Feb. 19)	(Air)		(Ankles, Calves Fluids-Intuition)	♂
XII	Pisces — (S)	Fish	Joel	Neptune	
	(Feb. 20-Mar. 20)	(Water)	James (Less)	(Feet — Psychic Faculty)	♀

TABLE "B" PLANETARY SIGNS — PLANETARY DIGNITIES

PLANET	MASC. FEM.	SYMBOL	RULES (Strength)	GLAND*	HOUSE	DETRIMENT (Loss of Power)	EXALTATION (Harmony)	FALL
Sun	♂	Fire	Leo		5	Aquarius	Aries	Libra
Mercury		Fire	Gemini Virgo	Pineal	3 6	Sagittarius Pisces	Gemini	Sagittarius
Venus	♀	Water	Taurus Libra	Thymus	2 7	Scorpio Aries	Pisces	Virgo
Moon	♀	Water	Cancer		4	Capricorn	Taurus	Scorpio
Mars	♂	Fire	Aries	Adrenals	1	Libra Taurus	Capricorn	Cancer
Jupiter		Fire	Sagittarius Pisces	Pituitary	9 12	Gemini Virgo	Cancer	Capricorn
Saturn		Earth	Capricorn Aquarius	Gonads	10 11	Leo Cancer	Libra	Aries
Uranus		Air	Aquarius	Thyroid	11	Leo	Scorpio	Taurus
Neptune		Water	Pisces	Lyden	12	Virgo	Leo	Aquarius
Pluto	♂	Fire	Scorpio		8	Libra	Aquarius	Leo

*Glandular relationships are noted as from the readings.

HOUSES

I **Personality** — Worldly outlook.
Head & Face.   Health, childhood, temperament.

II **Finances** — Gain or Loss.
Throat & Ears.   Liberty (Freedom)

III **Brethren** — Mental inclinations — Study — Writing — Short journeys.
Shoulders, Hands, Arms — Lungs, Nervous System, Relatives.

IV **Father** — Home, Environment — Lands, Property.
Breast, Stomach, Digestion.

V **Children** — Love Affairs, Emotions, Speculation, Games, Theatre.
Athletics & Sports.   Physical/Mental Joys.
Heart, Sides, Upper Back.

VI **Health** — Food, Hygiene, Clothing, Service (work).
Solar Plexus, Bowels.

VII **Personal Relationships** — Marriage, Partnerships, Contracts, Unions,
Open Enemies, etc.   (Partner's 1st House)
Kidneys, Ovaries, Veins, Lower Back.

VIII **Death** — Legacies, Astral Flight, Sex.
Muscles, Bladder, Loins, Sex Organs.

IX **Travel** — Education, Psychic Experiences, Philosophy, Religion.
Liver, Thighs.

X **Mother** — Profession or Occupation, Country or Government.
Knees.

XI **Friends** — Associations, Hopes & Wishes, Spiritual Joy.
Clubs, Societies, Humanitarian Work.
Ankles.

XII **Unseen or Unexpected Troubles** — Sorrows, Suffering, Secret Enemies.
Feet.   (Understanding) Charity, Sympathy, Hospitals, Penal Inst.

TABLE "D"

Houses — (Kinds)

Angular —   (1 - 4 - 7 - 10) Planets in these houses have greater
scope for dynamic action.

Succedent —   (Fixed — 2, 5, 8, 11) (After the Angular)
Planets in these tend to stability, purpose,
will power.

Cadent —   (3 - 6 - 9 - 12)
Adaptability, communication & ability to get along.

Houses of Life —   (1 - 5 - 9)
Houses of Endings —   (4 - 8 - 12)
Houses of Substance —   (2 - 6 - 10)
Houses of Relationships —   (3 - 7 - 11)

TABLE "E"

ZODIACAL SIGNS

TRIPLICITIES —

CARDINAL SIGNS — (Restless as in Angular Houses)	ARIES (Mars) Self	CANCER (Moon)	LIBRA (Venus) Mate	CAPRICORN (Saturn) Position
FIXED SIGNS — (Resist change)	TAURUS (Venus) Money	LEO (Sun)	SCORPIO (Mars) Sex	AQUARIUS (Saturn, Uranus) Wishes
MUTABLE/COMMON — (Adaptability)	GEMINI (Mercury) Mind to Matter	VIRGO (Mercury)	SAGITTARIUS (Jupiter) Law-Religion	PISCES (Neptune) Cause-Effect

QUADRUPLICITIES —

FIRE	EARTH	AIR	WATER
Aries	Taurus	Gemini	Cancer
Leo	Virgo	Libra	Scorpio
Sagittarius	Capricorn	Aquarius	Pisces

73

Glossary*

AKASHA — Soul record.

ANGLES — See Aspects.

ASCENDANT — That sign of the Zodiac (and degree) rising on the horizon at the moment of birth. (See Rising Sign.)

ASPECTS — Relationships, by angle or degree, of planets and zodiacal signs.
  Major Aspects are those considered most influential in an individual chart or horoscope. These include: (±5°) Conjunctions — 0°, Trines — 120°, Sextiles 60°, Oppositions — 180°, Squares 90°.

BIRTH CHART — Natal Chart or horoscope.

CABALISTIC — (R) Pertaining to the Cabala. Based on mystical methods of interpreting Scripture and foretelling the future.

CONSTELLATIONS — Groups of stars seen in the heavens. Those which overlap the Ecliptic (or great path of the sun) are those termed of the Zodiac; Aries, Taurus, Gemini, etc.

COSMIC INFLUENCES — (R) From the cosmos, or outer space; outside our own solar system.

CUSPS — That point or area where two signs of the Zodiac (or two houses) merge.

CYCLES — (R) See Ch. VI.

DEGREES — Signs of the Zodiac are measured in degrees (longitude) along the Ecliptic, 30° to each Sign. Planetary positions (noon of every day) can be found in Raphael's Ephemeris for the year where the noon position in degrees is given for each day. Sensitive degrees in a chart are those occupied by a planet or cut by an angle (aspect) of the chart. Mid-points between planets are also significant.

DESCENDANT — The point on the chart (or on the Ecliptic) exactly opposite (180°) the Ascendant.

DIMENSIONS — (R) A framework of mental relationships, (or "vibrations") eight in all — each represented by a planet. Example: Earth represents the third dimension.

ECLIPTIC — The great circle around which the Sun appears to travel in a year.
  Plane of the Ecliptic — The level on which the circle of the Ecliptic lies, projected to infinity. (Planes in general are the extension in space of any of the Great Circles.)

*Terms interpreted from or Generic to the readings are noted with an (R).

ENTITY — (R) See Soul-Entity.

ENVIRONS — (R) The readings use environs (accent on the "vi" syllable) almost exclusively to designate the soul's sojourns in planetary dimensions between earth lives, although sometimes the phrase "present environs" is used to mean present-life circumstances.

EQUINOX — "Equal night" at 0° Aries and 0° Libra. The beginning of Spring and Fall, or vernal/autumnal equinoxes.

ESOTERIC — (As in Astrology) Hidden or secret. Known only by the select or few.

FIXED STARS — So called because they are so distant from Earth that they maintain their relative positions and form recognizable constellations or groups of stars. An entire group may appear to rise or set owing to the rotation of the Earth on its axis. The further the group is from the Ecliptic the less it appears to move, until (Northern Hemisphere) the Pole Star (Polaris) remains as a fixed point and can be thought of as the hub of the Earth's orbit.

GEOCENTRIC — Considered as viewed from the Earth's center. Compare Heliocentric, as viewed from center of the Sun.

GREAT CIRCLE — Any circle, the plane of which passes through the center of the Earth.

HELIOCENTRIC — As viewed from the center of the Sun.

HOROSCOPE — The natal or birth chart and its relationship to the present incarnation.

HOUSES — Twelve in all. They number counterclockwise from the ascendant. (See Appendix)

I.C. — (Immum Coeli) Opposite the M.C. or Midheaven, 90° below the ascendant on a natal chart.

INNATE — (Latent) See Chapter I.

KARMA — (Law of) Cause and effect. Or, "As ye sow, so shall ye reap. As ye condemn, so are ye condemned. As ye forgive, so may ye be forgiven."

LATENT — Undeveloped, hidden or concealed.

MANIFESTED — A trait being developed or revealed.

MIDHEAVEN — (M.C.) The Zenith, 90° above the ascendant on a natal chart. Opposite I.C.

MYSTIC — (R) Spiritually significant or symbolic as pertaining to spirit, (not spiritualism) and the mysteries; a person believing in, or initiated into, the mysteries — By insight or immediate intuition in a state of spiritual ecstasy. (See occult.)

NADIR — Opposite the Zenith. (Not to be confused with I.C.)

NATAL CHART — Birth chart or horoscope.

OCCULT — (R) Mysterious; supernatural. Pertaining to the hidden sciences — magic, astrology, numerology, metaphysics, phenomenology, etc. (Not to be confused with mysticism. See Mystic & Spiritualism.)

PLANE — (R) A level of consciousness. There are said to be twelve in our solar system, symbolized by the Zodiac. (See Ecliptic)

PLANET — "Wanderer." A heavenly body which orbits around a central sun. (See Solar System.)

PROGRESSIONS — As in a "progressed" chart. Requires further calculations based on the natal chart which enable the astrologer to study the trends over a given period of time.

PSYCHIC FORCES — (R) Pertaining to the psychic, or soul; mental, spiritual aspects. (Conscious, subconscious, superconscious aspects combined.)

RISING SIGN — Due to the Earth's rotation our Sun appears to rise on the horizon. On the first full day of Spring, if we watch the sunrise we shall be viewing that section of the Zodiac known as Aries; a month later it will be Taurus, the next month Gemini, etc.
Two hours after sunrise (in Aries), Taurus will be rising; then Gemini two hours later, etc., until all twelve signs have risen above the horizon (each taking two hours) and we are greeted by another new day, again in Aries.

Therefore, twelve children, each born two hours apart on a single day, could have twelve different rising signs. (Along with twelve separate house arrangements governing the individual's planetary aspects.)

RULING PLANET — Each sign of the Zodiac has a planet said to be its ruler, or in affinity with it. (See Appendix II, Tables A & B)

SEPTIMUS — (R) A planet referred to in the readings prior to 1930 — Thought to be Pluto. (Author)

SIGNS — (See Zodiac)

SOJOURNS — (R) The readings refer to "sojourns in the earth," meaning the present and previous incarnations. They refer also to sojourns in planetary dimensions or planes of consciousness outside the earth. (Between lives) The word appearance or material (sojourns) is generally used for incarnations in the earth.

SOLAR SYSTEM
The Sun — Center of the Solar System. Self-luminous. The other Planets in the system shine in the reflected light of the Sun.
Diameter, 109 times that of Earth (865,400 miles).
Mass, 333,000 times that of Earth.
It rotates on its axis once every 25 days.

The Moon — A satellite of Earth. Its light, like that of the Planets, is reflected from the Sun.
Diameter, 2,160 miles.
Revolution round Earth, just over 27 days.
Rotation, once in every revolution, so that the same face is nearly always presented to the Earth.

Mercury — Nearest Planet to the Sun (36,000,000 miles).
Diameter, 3,000 miles.
Mass, 1/27th that of Earth.
Revolution round Sun, 88 days.
Rotation, only once in its circling of the Sun so that it always (or nearly) presents the same face to the Sun, as the Moon does to the Earth.

Venus — 67,000,000 miles from Sun.
Slightly smaller than Earth.
Revolution round Sun, 225 days.
Rotation period unknown with certainty.

Mars — 142,000,000 miles from Sun.
Diameter, half that of Earth (4,216 miles).
Mass, 1/9th that of Earth.
Revolution round Sun, 687 days.
Rotation period, 24½ hours.
It has two moons.

Jupiter — 483,000,000 miles from Sun.
Diameter, 87,000 miles.
Mass, 316 times that of Earth.
Revolution round Sun, 12 years.
Rotation, a little less than 10 hours.
It has eleven satellites or moons, some as distant from it as 20,000 miles. Two of these revolve in the opposite direction to the rest.

Saturn — 886,000,000 miles from Sun.
Diameter, 75,000 miles.
Mass, 95 times that of Earth.
Revolution round Sun, 29½ years.
Rotation, 10 hours.
Saturn has three rings composed of small particles. These lie in a plane inclined to the Ecliptic at about 28°. There are ten moons outside the rings, one of which is very small and moving in an opposite direction to the rest.

Uranus — 1,782,000,000 miles from Sun.
Diameter, 30,900 miles.
Mass, 15 times that of Earth.
Revolution round Sun, 84 years.

Rotation, 11 hours.

Uranus was discovered in 1781 by the astronomer Herschel. It has five satellites, four of which revolve in a plane perpendicular to the Ecliptic and in a retrograde direction.

Neptune — 2,793,000,000 miles from Sun.

Diameter, 32,000 miles.

Mass, 17 times that of Earth.

Revolution round Sun, about 165 years.

Rotation, 16 hours.

Neptune was discovered by Adams and Verrier in 1846. It has two satellites, one of which moves in a retrograde direction.

Pluto — About 3,670,000,000 miles from Sun.

Diameter, about the same as Mars.

Revolution round Sun, 248 years.

Discovered in 1930.

SOLSTICE (Latin: Sol or Sun; Sistere, to make stand.)

Summer solstice, approximately June 21st, when Sun enters the Sign of Cancer. Hence Tropic of Cancer, the demarcating line of the northern-most point on Earth where the Sun can be seen directly overhead. On or near December 22nd is the **Winter solstice,** when the Sun is directly overhead on the line of the Tropic of Capricorn and on this date Sun enters Capricorn. At these dates the Sun is at its farthest point from the Equator, or maximum declination, and we have the longest or shortest day of the year.

SOUL-ENTITY — (R) Q. "Does the soul-entity change in reincarnation?"

A. "The entity? The soul is the entity! The entity is the soul, and the mind and body of same, see? These only enter matter, or a new house, in incarnations." (1494-1)

SPHERES — (R) Combinations of planes and dimensions of consciousness.

SPIRITUALISM — The practice of communicating (or attempting to communicate) with spirits of the dead, usually through a medium.

TRANSITS — Present or projected inter-relationships (or angles) of the planets as they relate to the natal chart. See Ch. VI.

VIBRATIONS — (R) See p. 19

ZENITH — The midheaven, directly overhead. 90° above Ascendant, on a natal chart. Opposite nadir.

ZODIAC — (See Appendix II) A band of the heavens which extends 8° on either side of the Sun's apparent path. (Ecliptic) This circular band (360°) is divided into the twelve signs of the zodiac. (30° each)

Beginning with 0° Aries they bear the same names as the constellations lying in the band of the zodiac with which they will coincide approximately every 26,000 years.

NOTES

NOTES

NOTES

NOTES

NOTES

NOTES

NOTES

NOTES